THE SPIRIT OF
AGAPE SELF-HELP
FROM WITHIN

INSPIRATIONAL WRITINGS OF
TERRY HARVEY PH.D.

TERRY HARVEY PH.D.

Copyright © 2024 Terry Harvey PH.D.

All rights reserved. No part of this book may be reproduced, stored, or transmitted by any means—whether auditory, graphic, mechanical, or electronic—without written permission of both publisher and author, except in the case of brief excerpts used in critical articles and reviews. Unauthorized reproduction of any part of this work is illegal and is punishable by law.

ISBN: 979-8-89419-313-7 (sc)
ISBN: 979-8-89419-314-4 (hc)
ISBN: 979-8-89419-315-1 (e)

Because of the dynamic nature of the Internet, any web addresses or links contained in this book may have changed since publication and may no longer be valid. The views expressed in this work are solely those of the author and do not necessarily reflect the views of the publisher, and the publisher hereby disclaims any responsibility for them.

One Galleria Blvd., Suite 1900, Metairie, LA 70001
(504) 702-6708

For my darling husband, Michael
For my grandmothers: Luvenia and Ethel
For my darling children: Christopher, Aaron, Isaiah
Michael II, Jasmine, Ivory, Grace, and beloved Tikima

CONTENTS

Acknowledgments vii

Introduction ix

Chapter 1   Truth 1

Chapter 2   My First Experience in Meditation 17

Chapter 3   Patterns That People Develop During a Lifetime 25

Chapter 4   A Shift in Reality 41

Chapter 5   Conscious Thought 51

Chapter 6   The Word: Risen from the Dead 59

Chapter 7   Healing with Crystals and the Chakras 67

Chapter 8   Renewing of Your Mind into a New Birth ... 75

Chapter 9   I Am Today All That I Will Ever Be 81

Chapter 10   Others See Problems, I See Opportunity and Growth 89

Chapter 11   How Do I Know When My Higher Consciousness is talking to Me? 95

Chapter 12   The Quest: An Awakening 101

Chapter 13   Smudging and Cleansing Rituals 107

Chapter 14   A Transcendent Experience with the Infinite 111

Index 133

ACKNOWLEDGMENTS

I have gratitude:

To my friends, Loretta and Lamont, who have always been there for me.

To my sisters, Francine and Teanisha, for listening and loving me.

To my brother, Clarence (Stoney), who always has a good word for the day.

To my cousin, Eva, whose love and guidance helped give consciousness to this book.

To my spirit guides for all their input and guidance.

To Bob and Tobi, who have always been there for comfort when I needed a hug or a kiss.

INTRODUCTION

When I look back at that one day of true awakening, it kind of shocked my soul. I had gone for so long in a state of maybe, or I think I know, or faithful but doubtful. Oh what an oxymoron. This is how I lived in denial and pain and agony. My cousin Eva gave me some literature to read that was quite different from what I was used to reading. It kind of went against the grain of my traditionally taught religious dogma. I was protective of my embedded beliefs. After all, it was all I had to show for a lifetime of religious practices, rituals, and teachings.

My cousin was trying to help me regain control of my life. I had been living in seclusion for a number of years. The pain within my body had driven me away from family and friends. All attempts at faith healing and shallow prayer left me with no more than what I started with—more agony. My marriage was troubled, my children were stressed, and my responsibilities were overwhelming. I had taken an early retirement from the state for medical reasons and had resolved that my life was over. I stayed home—locked in my room—day after day except for the few times I ventured out to church. I enjoyed working in my garden alone. I enjoyed reading my Bible. I enjoyed interacting with my children. I didn't have many friends by choice, and I did not like to talk on the telephone. I was under a lot of stress, according to my psychiatrist, but I did not see it at all. I was blind to all the problems that were weighing my Spirit down.

My doctors had been requesting that I move south for many years. I was told that my health would be a lot better. Finally relenting, I moved the whole gang to rural Florida.

There was no change in my health at the time. Eva said, "I think that I can help you."

I said, "Oh, really?"

She explained that she had a gift that she had received from the Holy Spirit; it involved healing with her hands. I told her that I needed a real healer—not a faith healer—because I had tried the faith healer. It had not worked for me; it only discouraged me.

She said, "I understand."

After numerous books on the subject of mediums, psychic abilities, mysticism, and metaphysics, we began our healing sessions. My doctors had already told me that I was truly depressed and needed medication. What was this depression? Why was I depressed? Why was I even sick? It was all far from my understanding. I only knew that most of the time I used a walker just to get around the house. I was in agony at all times. I used the motor chair to do my shopping at the grocery store. My grandmother cared for me throughout the day. I was ashamed.

All the while, I had the power of creating my own life experiences right there inside of me. I had the power to heal my life. I just did not know how to access this power from within. It was there that my journey began.

The Holy Spirit is among us and is always connected to us and all energy within the universe. We have heard this statement countless times. Nonetheless, how many people actually believe this to be true? It is believed by many religious leaders—as well as followers—that divine beings were part of the universal makeup long before this world we even created. It is believed that these spirit beings have been endowed with a job by the Infinite to assist mankind in his life while he inhabits this physical flesh on earth. The spirit of the Infinite is connected to all living creatures and matter. The Infinite, being pure perfect energy, flows through all. It created all from self.

There is a universal law in this dimension in which we live that implies that if we think it, we can ultimately create it. What would happen if you could actually hear, communicate, and see the spirit? Would this new knowledge change one's perception of death and life? What if you received a gift from the Holy Spirit of vision—but you really did not want it?

How could you continue to walk the earth blind? Could you continue to pretend that life after death did not exist? Or would this new knowledge destroy your psychological makeup and leave you catatonic? Our inner spirit is the most resilient, empowering, and most real aspect of one's being. It is amazing that we are all caught up in the dogmatic realm of religious philosophy.

This is truly a self-help book for the ages. To read this book is to be empowered in the alembic of change within self and connecting with the power of the Infinite one. The knowledge from this book is empowering one to change with knowledge and super natural insight connecting one to God. Here one will learn the core of each being. This core is the energy of infinite, self-creative intelligence within the universe. We are therefore, all infinite within time. We are creative in thought and mind—and connected to all. Consciously or unconsciously, we form life through thought.

My life changed unpretentiously and unassuming of others. I learned to let go of self. All that I felt and knew from within became real to me. I began to meditate daily. Meditation allowed the spirit to fully engulf my soul's potential. Shortly thereafter, I began to learn about energy healing and prosperity manifestation. Meditation served as an entrance into the soul in which I lived. It allowed me to hear and see me within the God within me. Meditation helped me empty the vessel of my mind, leaving room for spirit to enter. The mind is so busy with the clutter of the day that it is almost impossible for spirit to enter such a chaotic place. By going into a meditative state, the room can be cleared as you sit before the altar of honor and praise.

All of my life, I have been gifted to see and feel spirits. Nonetheless, my gift was feared during those years due to prejudiced teachings and religious control. Michael Bernard Beckwith said, "I have experienced spiritual liberation." And it feels so good. I feel so alive, so in tune with the Holy Spirit, so prosperous, so generous, so forgiving of all, and so loving. I really get it now. I really see the light from within. Many of you do not believe in survival of consciousness after death; many of you believe but are afraid to admit it due to your own religious convictions. The dogmatic structure in our society leaves so many of us in confusion that it is impossible for the heart to smile at the truth without fear of man.

In this book, you can relax your soul and your mind. You will find solitude to be at peace as you expand your wisdom. This self-help book is filled with optimism and challenges designed to foster strength in your convictions as you evolve into the new, highly conscious individual you already are. You just have to find yourself. You are all that you will ever be. It is all waiting for you to discover it. It already exists and always has existed. There are no solutions for time in our space. We just need to find the door to access it and make it our own.

I have written this book in order to reveal the truth to those that are afraid of the unknown and the condemnation of others. I have written it for those who straddle the fence in their beliefs but have seen and heard just as I have seen and heard. I have written it for those who need to be told that their minds can actually change their worlds. Their thoughts and actions are all creative—whether they believe it or not.

I grew up a Baptist in a family that was terribly fearful of the hailing of fire and brimstones; it was hard to look for the truth. To find the truth means finding death or rejection. It means isolation and being labeled a witch or a voodoo princess among African American people. I have written this book to save all those who want to know the truth and find liberation within their own spirits.

It is clear that we are a spiritual people. We are constantly evolving into a new consciousness. Believing in ourselves as the Infinite dwells within us, we are moving and transforming the power of love and devotion to a God that we can communicate with—and not just talk to. To feel free to think and practice one's beliefs without retribution or retaliation from the dogmatic rhetoric system that engulfs us daily.

This book helps to show that we—as an evolved people—do not need a leader to show us the way to our infinite calling. We have an intelligent spirit dwelling within us. We may access this power whenever we need it for all things are positive within the universe. The Word is within your own mouth—all one has to do is speak it. Nonetheless, if you must have a leader to help you through this evolutionary process and steady the course, do what is best for you. Remember to donate to this leader for his time and services, but do not try to pay him for salvation because that he has not. Salvation belongs to the Lord, and we will all see home if our lifestyle is of praise, honor, and love for all. Spirit lives forever. One has a choice where to spend eternity—and in whose company in spirit.

If I can show nothing else within this book, I hope to show the power of thought. This power, which is part of a universal law, is greater than all the words one can come up with within a day. Thought has power—whether one believes it or not—and it has power and is forever creating good or bad for the thinker.

It is important to always have positive thoughts. If we speak it, we create it. We can create the health we desire, the prosperity in our lives that we desire, and the happiness, love, forgiveness, and peace we so desperately need and want. We just have to learn to think positively as we go into that little room—which really is very large in contrast—and meditate. Empty the glass in order that spirit may have room to fill it.

Take a quiet meditative thought—in the morning, during meditation, or in the evening—and hold this thought in silence: "Let the words of thy mouth and the meditation of thy heart be acceptable in the Lord's sight, O Jehovah, my rock, and my redeemer."

This scripture comes from the Holy Bible. It opens the door to your heart through thoughts of the infinite. For example, the words in your mouth and the thoughts of one's heart will begin to mold the spiritual substance into manifestation within one's life.

Open the door to all possibilities of positive living and good by thinking of him in honor and obedience. If our thoughts are in balance with the infinite, we can create a vibration so high within the spiritual realm that whatever is thought of is immediately created.

TRUTH

I affirm that there is but one truth.
I affirm that we are all connected through love.
I affirm that the spirit of the Infinite dwells within me.

The first thing I would like to do is define religion as the discovery of truth. Truth is defined as an awakening of the mind to become free to listen to the inner voice within. Truth gives us the strength to escape the fear of rejection, doubt, sickness, poverty, and the narrow confines of embedded religious beliefs. I define religious as the rituals associated with religion. Restraints are used to control the services and beliefs of the people that practice various religions. We must dare to eliminate mundane religious practices and dogmas that hinder the awakening of our minds to the truth. The only truth is one path, one ultimate source of energy, one infinite in reality.

I try not to use the word "God" too often. The word "God" has been so misinterpreted that it actually limits our experience of our higher power rather than expanding it. Therefore, you will hear me say Infinite One, Higher

Consciousness, Energy Source, I Am, or many other superior names for the "One that is All" more than the traditional word "God."

The discovery of truth is a result of deep meditation and expressing enlightened consciousness through active daily living. This enlightenment is no more than an awakening of our inner God-Mind that has been with us from the very beginning of life. Simply put, everything that we need has been put in place within the universe and within our spirits. Spiritual law is just waiting for the opportunity to be activated through self-awareness or a higher consciousness. Discovering the truth will allow one to live a more productive, healthier, and more prosperous life. Discovering the truth will allow one to help self from within. It can open the pill bottle of spirituality and awaken one to a whole new world of living. This truth will allow one to become true to self and the ultimate source of energy.

Jesus the Christ made all of this very clear in the Holy Bible. The Holy Bible is not the only inspired holy book written through inspiration of the Holy Spirit. It's just the one that I am using to reference from at this time; to find the healer within, we must invest in what we do not know. Most people only invest in what they know or think they know. It is difficult to alter old ground in religious traditions or beliefs. You may find it easier to chop a redwood tree down with only an ax.

My job is to help you open up to what you do not know but think that you know and what you cannot see but ultimately feel in your spiritual guidance system. To help you get past all these ingrained fear-based ideologies and misconceptions of the truth. To find the healer, we must access the unseen world of spirit. When it comes to matters that peer into the vastness of life and being, we can be pretty sure that what we think we know, we have a lot more to learn on the subject. I do know that 99 percent of the unseen world is reality, but we place 99 percent of our undivided attention upon the seen world. When we access the unseen, we access the eternal energy of the ultimate energy source.

You can help yourself as well as others access it by being comfortable, familiar, and valuing, honoring, and knowing the spirit for yourself. No matter how much we think that we know or understand the laws and the workings of the human soul and the spirit and all the unseen realms, we are really only touching on the edge of this knowledge. Some have more knowledge than others—and some have more of a connection than others—but all have some. When we influence the unseen world through thought, we influence the seen world.

There is another word that I would like to define. That word is mysticism. My professor Dr. Leon Masters gave many definitions for that one word. Dr. Leon Masters is the founder of the University of Metaphysics and the University of Sedona. The one that best defines mysticism in my mind is: "To make direct contact with the Supreme Universal Intelligence Mind—or God—in the deeper levels of the human mind, in order to synthesize the daily functional mind with the creative intelligence of the universe, thus enabling one to create one's life as one desires."

If we are to grow spiritually, we must leave the infancy stage of biblical interpretation and enter a spiritual adulthood. This has everything to do with living up to our innate potentials. It is about daring to become attuned with the higher energy source or "I Am." We are all growing in this spiritual evolutionary process. Whether we allow ourselves to grow or stunt our spiritual growth with blindfolds over our minds or plugs in our ears, the choice is ours and ours alone.

There have been many well-known enlightened individuals over the ages. Buddha, Guru Nanak, Muhammad, Gandhi, Laozi, Jesus Christ, and the Dalai Lama are just a few. Each awakening provides an individualized navigation to the same ultimate energy source. We are all in this evolutionary process, moving at different speeds with our own time-tables. All roads lead home. However, it is important to remember that home is where the heart is. I believe Jesus said, "Where your treasure is, so shall your heart be also." - Luke 12:34

We are all alike in the sense that we desire the same things. For instance, we are all seeking the joy of living and prospering. We all want to be needed and loved unconditionally, we want complete wellness and health, and we want to be a part of the excitement of life. I believe that this is a desire in all living things. Evolution is undisputable proof that life aspires to a process of continual growth—both spiritually and physically. Therefore, I must ask a question: How do we come to know the truth?

Historically, humankind has employed four methods to acquire knowledge. These methods are rationalism, intuition, authority, and the scientific method. I chose to pursue truth with intuition, rationalism, and the scientific method. I did not use authority because I would have to believe that something is considered true because of tradition or because some person of distinction says that it is true. I wanted to be more "absolute" in my knowing.

When I rationalize, I use reasoning to conclude my knowledge. I assume that if the premises are sound and the reasoning is carried out according to the rules of logic, then the conclusion will yield the absolute truth. I use this method a lot while raising my children. It has never failed me.

Intuition is my first tool of choice when seeking truth and guidance. When I talk of intuition, I'm referring to the sudden insight, clarifying idea, or thought that springs forth from our consciousness all at once. Intuition usually springs forth after reasoning has failed. It is more like a sudden flash of knowledge that springs forth from the mind emphatically—without any evidence to back it up. It is a metaphysical process that we have the most rudimentary knowledge of.

When I look into the scientific method for establishing truth, I am relying on an objective assessment. Nonetheless, I am still using reasoning and intuition, but I'm establishing a hypothesis about some feature in our reality. I might even go as far as establishing and experimenting to objectively test my hypothesis. As a metaphysician, I have used all of the methods mentioned.

I soundly walked soul and mind first into Christian Spiritualism through meditation, education, and prayer. Christian Spiritualism is the belief in Christ with the philosophy, characteristics, and a system of thought that affirms the existence of immaterial reality imperceptible to the senses of man. According to the world religions book second edition, "Spiritualist believe there are other planes of existence for example, the next higher plane is similar to this earthly one but operates at a higher rate of vibration and luminosity". Through prayer and affirmations, I was enlightened through Thought and the Holy Spirit. I was given the ability to see and hear the spirit world much clearer. I was shown through the spirit how to use my thoughts to co-create my reality. The spirit overflowed my soul with love, forgiveness, healing, wellness, prosperity, generosity, and the knowledge that all I had to do was ask and it would be given. The spirit of the God within touched my soul, endowing me with wisdom. I have the power within me to heal, prosper, and do all things through the power of our ultimate source. I have been blessed with the perfect self-help from within from all the knowledge instilled within me.

Stand for Your Beliefs

From the beginning of time, mankind has had revelations, awakenings, and enlightenment from a higher energy source. Many people have become self-actualized but refused to acknowledge the truth due to fear of ridicule or financial retribution. We often sit in silence, afraid of judgment from our elders, society, friends, relatives, and dogma established by religious leaders within our community and altered religious scriptures. Perhaps you dare to share your own thinking out loud as I have for many years due to fear of personal persecutions.

Maybe I thought other people would think I was pathological or I was going against God. Dogma has hindered so many from the truth. The Bible states that the penalty for anyone practicing mediumship among the Israelites was death (Leviticus 20:27, NIV).

Leviticus 19:31 (NIV) states, "Do not turn to mediums or seek out spiritists for you will be defiled by them." Statements such as these—made by man to control the masses—have led to unfounded fear, anger, and disbelief.

People have to remember that "man" wrote the Bible through divine inspiration from the Holy Spirit. When you are dealing with anything that man does, one has to remember that man will always put a part of himself into the mix. Even though the Bible clearly states that no one should add or take away from the Holy Scripture, it is clear that there have been tremendous changes with additions and deletions.

Have you ever heard of the Lost Scriptures? They do exist. Some were lost, and others were removed. Also, during the Council of Nicaea (AD 325), many changes took place in Christian belief, practice, and worship. It is my understanding through extensive research that the Council of Nicaea marked the beginning of the end of the truth. Christians could no longer believe in preexistence, reincarnation, or salvation through a union with God in the Christian doctrine. Of course, this council was made up of holy men. Constantine, in particular, thought he was a god. It appears to me that he molded Christianity in his own image and made Jesus the only Son of God. Maybe he meant well in the beginning of his quest, but power changes even the best intentions of people. It took more than 200 years for some of these changes in Christianity to be removed.

It is important to gather our thoughts and go back to research the beginning. Who wrote the Holy Scripture? How was it passed down before being translated and put on paper or stone? What were some of people's problems during that era? Who had power and control when the Holy Scripture was written? Who had control when decisions were being made to put certain gospels in the Holy Bible? Why were some gospels put in the Bible—and others were not? Do the things that were said make sense or sound credible? Why were so many Christians persecuted? Do these persecutions sound like something a perfect God would want man to participate in? What is this heresy? Didn't God give man free will? I petition you people of the world! Awaken! Awaken! Awaken!

The Gospel According to Mary Magdalene

This particular gospel was intentionally left out of the Bible. It is unclear why it was not included. It could have been because women had no respect from others—even though today she is considered an apostle. Could it be because she spoke of a spiritual ascension or the indwelling God within the mind? She spoke of the soul and its work against negative or evil energy. For some reason, the church leaders during the time the Bible was put together found that what she had to say did not quite mesh with what they wanted the people to understand or know. Here again, man put his feelings or beliefs in the mix, refusing to relay the divine message given to a woman.

The ultimate source is still revealing to us today. Does God tell us that what we hear is correct or altered far from the truth? I believe that Christ came to help us get it right through the spirit. I believe that man has altered and changed so much for his own self-control and gratification that man has become devout and pious. There is a pious fraud in those whose beliefs are more devoted to what man says than what the Holy Spirit reveals to the heart and mind. I also believe that it is sanctimonious to condemn other people's beliefs by using their actions as a mask for personal immorality.

In the early days of my enlightenment, I doubted my own awakening to the truth. I questioned every aspect of discovery. I searched for confirmation of truth in spirit and materialization. I had to learn through confirmation from the Holy Spirit that "All" was as real as the ground that I stood upon. I want to encourage you to dare to be you—and dare to stand for your beliefs. Do not hide behind closed doors or dismiss your revelations of the true "God Mind Within." Our bodies are God's temples. If our bodies are to house the supreme source, then God dwells within us. When we become open to this consciousness, it becomes impossible to remain so caught up with self-gratification or today's dogmatic doctrine. To become truly able to help ourselves, we need only to learn, to set aside the self, and become true enough to depend on the spirit. At times, we may feel awkward or even look a little demented for the love of the Holy Spirit. One thing that we must always remember is that truth is always truth. It never has to be contemplated or remembered—it will always be the same.

We are Connected through Spirit

From my university studies, scriptural texts, and mystical life experiences, it is clear that we are all connected to the infinite one. When we view the scriptures of various religions, we see various degrees of enlightenment or awakening that depend on the evolutionary process of human time and space. When we examine the core of all messages given through divine inspiration, enlightenment, or true awakening, there are very few differences or contradictions. The five major religions all believe in one ultimate God. For Instance, Hindus believe in Brahman, but he has many names and faces. The average Catholic or lay Christian has no knowledge of this information. We are taught at an early age to disapprove of other religions without any true knowledge of them. We take the advice and unfounded sermons of our traditional Christian or Muslim ministers as gospel. We accept their interpretations of our religious scriptures and texts as divine inspiration. This interpretation always seems to divide humanity and its religious beliefs.

It is not hard to open your minds and hearts to understanding that sometimes we get it wrong. The infinite is as perfect as perfection can possibly be conceived. He created all from self—with unending love for humanity. Having said that, how is it possible that he could tell Christians to kill in his name due to a difference in beliefs or instruct Muslims to kill in his name as a war on those that are different. We all worship the ultimate source by whichever name we choose to call him.

There is but one ultimate source of energy in which we call God. Islam calls him Allah. Christians call him

"I Am," and some teach of the Trinity, yet he is one God. Buddhism teaches the concept of Anatman or "no self." Their ultimate goal is to attain nirvana. For them, the Brahman, the universal soul, and understanding that Brahman brings enlightenment are all that exists. Hinduism teaches of Brahman (ultimate reality) and Atman (the self), yet Sikhs believe in one God (Waheguru). The Sikhs believe that God is not Muslim or Hindu. They believe that God is not defined by any one religion. God is called by many different names.

Moses asked, "Lord, whom shall I say sent me?"

God responded, "Tell them that I Am that I Am sent you."

This statement in itself is evident that God is all. Based on a few cultural beliefs, language barriers, and regions in the world, we have come up with different names for the same spirit—a spirit that connects us all to the ultimate source.

Many mystics over the years have tried to teach the true knowledge of one God. They all stand in agreement that there is but one true source of energy. This energy is the life force present in all that there is within the universe. This energy has been communicating with us throughout the ages. It gives us what we can handle—no more and no less—as we evolve spiritually.

New Thought Beliefs

I believe that the universe is a huge, multidimensional connection of influences, knowledge, light, energy patterns, electromagnetic fields, and matter. Everything is connected, and everything we do is somehow linked to everything else. Nothing separates man from anything else but his thinking.

My belief brings me to the most controversial concept of the New Age philosophy. Many believe that God dwells or lives within; therefore, we—as humans—are part of God. Since the belief says that there is no separateness, we are each godlike; God, therefore, is in each of us. As we experience God through our spirit, God experiences through us. Basically what is being said is that we are made up of God's energy. Because of this power that we possess, we can create whatever we want in our reality. Since we are all co-creators with God's energy, the energy that makes the universe dwells within.

How do we sort out these multilayered levels of beliefs and their perceptions? I believe the spirit is motivating new approaches to the truth in science and on television today. It is almost impossible to turn on TV without seeing a program on the paranormal, ghost hunters, psychics, or anything dealing with reality shows or the afterlife. My belief is that we do not have to sort out anything. As a people or spirits, we create our own reality for eternity. The Bible is the largest book ever written through divine inspiration of the Holy Spirit—or mediums and psychic individuals. Some would say I am blasphemous. Others would bless me for having the courage to speak the truth. Bless you for having the nerve and strength to request the Infinite to send "self, even if it means going alone." It is time to stop living a lie. If you believe in ghost, spirits, or even the Bible being written through divine inspiration of the Holy Spirit or God, you believe in psychics or mediums channeling information and prophets. You will have to learn to dismiss the lies added to the Holy Scripture to control your thoughts, actions, and beliefs.

If you are accustomed to living in constant communion with the infinite—and truly enjoy the transforming touch of the spirit—there is no truth greater than the awakening of your soul as countless as it may be. There is no intellect than can convince you that the universal source is not real. There can be no convincing that what you have heard and seen with your own ears, eyes, and mind is not real.

I had a transcendent experience with the infinite. There can be no turning back now. I have walked the warm sandy beaches with the Holy Light. I have warmed my spine in the healing light of Source Energy. I have walked hand in hand through the green valleys of home with the one I recognize as Christ. I have experienced the total euphoric feeling of love and healing in the light.

What Man Wants

I believe that we are searching for the aid of the Holy Spirit to heal our infirmities, our minds, and our lives to give us the secret to prosperity. People really have no desire for a higher consciousness. They have wedged themselves into place that is all about the "me." They want to continue the lust of the physical world and the vitality of the spirit at the same time; they are in a state of wanting their cake and eating it too. It is time to learn that indulgence in bodily pleasures is detrimental to success in life. We must learn that we must die daily as a sacrifice unto the God Within if we are to prosper or enjoy perfect health and vitality. There are always consequences for indulgence of appetite and passion.

Whomever we call the ultimate source should be honored daily as we go about his business. One of the secrets to life is to use all our substance in life in the most exalted way. If one would turn over one's life in covenant to the Supreme Being—seeking first the kingdom of God—all things shall be added unto them. Our Supreme Being has built in a materializing mechanism within the universe to meet our needs. He has given us the power of "thought." He has given us a universal law.

The Bible says, "In the beginning, the Word was with God, and the Word was God." All things that were made were made by him; without him, nothing was made that was made. It is understood that at the very beginning of creation was the Word, which is spirit or God. We must understand that the Word is idea, concept, manifestation, or thought that is infinite. It speaks itself into existence. God inevitably speaks, and it is done.

Therefore, everything that spirit thinks must take a form. I am trying to relay the message to you that we live in a universe of infinite substance and form. Nothing is created in any way unless infinite intelligence first thinks it. If we can believe it, we can receive it. Therefore, if we can apply thought to any need, idea, desire, or belief system, we can co-create our reality. Our bodies—as the temple of God—allow the Almighty that dwells within us and is connected to all life to work in accordance with the law of the universe, which is co-creating with God. In other words, we can have what we want if we just learn how to use thought in the process of manifestation.

"Most of the time, when we don't see the things that we've requested, we get frustrated. We get disappointed. And we begin to become doubtful. The doubt brings about a feeling of disappointment. Take that doubt and shift it. Recognize that feeling and replace it with a feeling of unwavering faith, and know that it is on the way.

—**Lisa Nichols**

MY FIRST EXPERIENCE IN MEDITATION

I affirm that I am in a continual eternal connection.
I affirm that all energy is infinite.

My first meditative experience was very discouraging. It seemed impossible to quiet my mind long enough to focus within. My intent was to use meditation as a tool for self-realization. I was attempting to use underlining yoga during meditation to assist in the awakening of the energy from the base of my spine to the top of my head. Things were not working out as I planned. I knew that it took a lot more than one day of meditation to learn to focus, quite my mind, and go into a trance.

I was going through a process of becoming a sage as I grew in age. As I grew in wisdom, I wanted to become more spiritual and connect with the ultimate Source. Day after day, I practiced meditation, prayed, and chanted. I sat with my feet flat on the floor, arms outward, opened my chakras, starting at the base of my spine: Remember to breathe, Terry. Okay, they are open. Protect myself with white protective light of God, okay. Remember to take deep breaths as you count them. When was I supposed to take the car to the shop? Oh that's not until later in the day. Oh my goodness, I didn't fix Isaiah's lunch for his trip today. Oh no—I'm off track. Clear my mind. Count your breaths, Terry. You can do this.

Learning to control your thoughts in order to clear your mind is a process. It is impossible for the Holy Spirit to enter a place that has no room for it. For instance, if a glass is already full, there is no room for spirit. One must be willing to let go of self and empty the mind of all clutter. This practice will open up the mind to receive a clearer channel from spirit. It is already hard enough to distinguish the voice from self and the enemy. When we say that "God said" or "the Holy Spirit revealed," shouldn't one be sure of the voice or the nudging was actually from the ultimate source?

Meditation will help when discerning the voice or guidance of God. It allows you to empty all thoughts and clutter from your mind. It allows one to open a channel from distractions. Imagine talking on the phone and the signals from the cell phone tower get crossed. You not only hear the person that you are talking to—but two or three other people at the same time. You would have to hang up and call back because you can't really understand anything being said. What you think you heard is not really what was said at all. This is when wrong information is given out to the masses and interpretations are questioned.

The channel needs to be clear in order to hear. Self needs to be set aside; the goal is to help honor him and help mankind. If one can pierce the veil of appearances, one can become a part of reality. In order to heal one's life from within, it is important to establish the daily discipline of mediation. This discipline will lead to a life of freedom and true spiritual liberation.

Michael Bernard Beckwith said, "Transformation occurs when identification with the egoist self is dropped through a conscious realization of the authentic self."

In truth, we must first go through a mental cleansing. This cleansing will ultimately free the self, allowing one to become self-actualized. Allow the self to feel the oneness with the ultimate source of life.

Establishing a Spiritual Substance through Meditation

When we meditate, we establish the spiritual body in our consciousness. This body, according to the Christ, was not made by hands. It was eternal in the heavens. Through meditation, we are able to gain strength and spiritual power. This power is transmitted to our physical bodies. Anything we touch or that comes into our vibration empowers us in the physical and material world.

Some Christians believe the practice of eastern meditation enhances a person's sensitivity to the spirit world, enabling them to acquire the ability to channel spirits. Channeling is a divination method that has been used throughout history. I do not know if this idea is factual. Most mediums believe a person has to be born with the gift of channeling or mediumship. Even though one can be taught during meditation to channel or contact spirits, a person can only go as far as their gift allows. As I stated earlier in this book, all people are gifted to a certain degree with psychic ability. Others are gifted with an ordained amount of psychic ability from birth. Some embrace their God-given gifts, and others see it as a transgression and dismiss it altogether.

As I studied the religious material concerning mediums and prophets, I discovered that religious leaders and spiritual followers are the same. They use different names to do the same work, prayers, or meditations. The prophets speak words of wisdom from the Holy Spirit, and so do the medium and the minister. The prophet or minister would say that the information is coming from God, and the medium would say that the information is coming from a spirit or a deceased person, which is still a spirit from God. They speak of information from angels, guides, and the Holy Spirit. I have yet to hear a medium state that their knowledge came from something evil or Satan.

I see people trying to control the masses through religious beliefs. If the old Christian Orthodox could get the people to come to them for answers and help instead of "I Am," they could control the people and kill those that did not go along with the program.

"I will set my face against the person who turns to mediums and spiritists to prostitute himself by following them. I will cut them off from his people" (Lev. 20:6, NIV).

Joan of Arc is considered a saint by Roman Catholics. When she spoke of voices that told her what do, she was considered to be consorting with the devil by the same type of Christians that ordained her with sainthood. The poor young woman was burned at the stake due to no fault of her own. Going against any religious teaching used to be a death sentence.

However, today, one may only be ostracized from immediate family or be called a witch. My grandmother is a die heart southern Baptist. She believes in nothing new. Anything new is blasphemous. Yet the preacher can stand in the pulpit every Sunday morning and tell her thus said the Lord. He can tell her of his revelation and what God said directly to him. But when I tell her what the Holy Spirit said to me, I am considered blasphemous. This is only fear on her part and so many others. Fear of the unknown. Fear to reject what our ancestors put in writing to control the masses. Fear that in some way they may be rejecting God.

The more I meditated, the more freedom I began to experience within my life. The more I meditated, the more open my mind became to intuitive guidance from the Holy Spirit. The more I meditated, the more validation I received from the spirit within. It is a spirit of newness and life. It is a spirit of prosperity, generosity, health, love, happiness, forgiveness, and peace. I cannot explain the overwhelming feeling of love and joy that I feel when the spirit is upon me.

Empty your mind and become attuned to the Holy Spirit. Seek a spiritual liberation from the confines of modern-day super-churches and mega-ministers. Become one with the infinite and speak to him directly for yourself. Experience abundance, perfect health, happiness, love, joy peace, and forgiveness without feelings of betrayal. Access your wealth from within. Begin to live up to your full potential.

While it is great to be generous, you must know that your prosperity does not depend upon how much you give to the churches or ministers. Generosity comes in time as well as money. While it is a requirement from the Holy Spirit to help others in as many ways as possible, it is not a requirement to be blind to financial abuse. If your pastor is driving a Bentley or a Mercedes and the congregation can barely pay their rent, there is surely an imbalance within the ministry. The people are not getting what they need spiritually to grow—and the money is not being allocated to the needy as the true "I Am" intended.

I do not believe that Jesus drove the best chariots and wore the best silk. He used his resources to help others in every way. He made sure that there was always a sufficient supply in the warehouse to help others—whether they were a member of his congregation or not. Some of us do not need leaders to spend our money for us or to show us how to use our finances. Others are in desperate need for a leader to listen to the voice within. They have not learned to listen to the God within, and they seek others to do it for them.

There is nothing wrong with having a leader help one access the truth. There is nothing wrong with the pastor receiving a salary from the church, but there should be a balance of wealth if it is earned through the church. When does one grow up in the spirit in order to see truth? How many years does it take to evolve into a state of receptiveness to the Holy Spirit? It does not take a degree or a supernatural event to become awakened. It only takes daily meditation and prayer.

This simple exercise of meditation, faithfully performed daily, will awaken the soul to an abundance of being alive without need. I am attempting to teach one to awaken the "Selfless Self" as described by Buddhists or "Supreme Self" according to the Hindus. These are lessons of liberation from the confines of modern dogma. Such liberation will enable one to remain free throughout life in prosperity, love, and happiness. Despite what happens in life or death, joy shall be yours eternally.

"Each of us comes to the awareness of the truth in her or his own way. Some of our lessons are easily learned: others are incredibly difficult. But we are all expanding our knowledge of ourselves and the meaning of life all the time. There are lessons on wealth, lessons in poverty, in victory, defeat, and physical challenges. We are daughters and sons of God. We, too, are divine. Each and every experience is an encouragement to have faith in our divinity, to strive to achieve higher consciousness, which is the purpose of our journey."

—Susan L. Taylor

PATTERNS THAT PEOPLE DEVELOP DURING A LIFETIME

I affirm that the presence of spirit is within me.
I affirm that the presence of spirit
blesses everyone I meet.
I affirm that the presence of spirit heals
everything and everyone I touch.
I affirm that the presence of spirit brings gladness into my life.
I affirm that my spirit is free to love
unconditionally, releasing all negativity

You may have established a belief within your mind that all this metaphysical, spiritual mysticism or religious doctrine is okay, but you really do not believe in any of it wholeheartedly. There is something inside you that tells you that maybe God is real—but maybe he isn't. First of all, I must inform you that the little voice that speaks of the negative is the enemy. His greatest accomplishment is to convince you that our Supreme Being does not exist.

As you can see, I will leave the subject at times to express ideas that need to be brought out at that moment.

For sure, this is a deliberate change of subject on my part and should not to be confused with inconsistency. The Holy Spirit has inspired me to write this inspirational self-help book. I must write and speak as it moves me.

Patterns of negative thought and actions that are developed over a lifetime can—and may—hinder one from becoming all that he or she desires in this universe. The thought process can hinder the quality of our lives and have severe negative impacts on our finances and health. Remember that we are co-creators of our reality. If we can be honest with ourselves, we will admit that we have established set patterns and routines since birth. These patterns and routines follow us throughout our lives. Their impact is detrimental. When we become conscious of these negative patterns, we can alter them as needed through constant training of the mind. Have you ever discovered how hard it is to break a bad habit? Negative thoughts and patterns have exactly the same resistance to change.

Evolved Persons

An evolved person recognizes these faults through prayer, meditation, and observation of one's life. The evolved person uses these negative thoughts and actions by making them into positives. The Divine God-Within—the temple of the evolved person's body—can heal the body, allowing the right conditions to exist for healing to take place. Your thoughts can manifest prosperity, love, a sound mind, and the strength to do all things through your ultimate source.

When one becomes evolved, it is inherent to give gratitude to the Supreme Being. When we finally escape these negative thoughts and patterns and recognize the ultimate universal intelligence and energy, we become enlightened or awakened. We become evolved through this process. We develop gratitude at that stage. We give thanks for life—and for the universe itself. We give thanks for what most people take for granted. That is why some monks pray six times a day, some Christians pray throughout the day, and some Muslims pray three times a day. Gratitude is simply an expression of true humility. It is an acknowledgement of faith in all that our Supreme Being said he would do.

When we shed the burdens of complaints, shallow beliefs, self-pity, and total mental blockage of the concept of abundance, we can begin to live as the Supreme Being intended us to live. Anyone desiring to heal their physical life and their spiritual life must stop seeing, reading, listening to, or even conversing about illness, financial instability, negative relationships, and the downright lack of anything that is desired. We must replace the negative with the positive. Our thinking must be positive at all times. Our belief in the infinite power to do as he said he would do must be practiced in our daily lives. We must live and act as though we are healed. We must talk as if we are already healed. From my experience, your desires and beliefs must be a vibrational match in order to be manifested.

Manifestation

The concept of manifestation relies of the assumption that like attracts like. That which is like unto itself draws the same unto itself. The vibration of your thoughts must match all your desires if you intend to manifest your desires into your reality. You cannot desire something and totally focus on the absence of it. This concept acts totally against the laws of the universal plan. Your desires and beliefs must be a vibrational match if you are to receive your desires and your god-given favor from the ultimate source. We tend to develop negative habits in relation to our daily living practices. We say one thing—but believe something very different. We practice one way and say something as different as the sun and the stars. You must first understand that you are a vibrational transmitter. You are energy, electrical currents, and vibrations within the universe. You possess the power to co-create your reality. Our bodies are the temple of God; therefore, we are part infinite energy. The infinite one takes no part in confusion. Our thoughts must be true—and our actions must be in harmony with our beliefs.

The secret to manifestation is that you must live as though all your desires have been met by the infinite source. In reality, they have already been met. God does not work on the premise of time. Only humans work on this timeline. What he said he would do, he did a long time ago—before we were even thought of. He is only waiting for us to manifest our desires into our lives.

This manifestation comes through acting out, living, and believing as though it is already done. Sometimes we have to use imagination to get the ball rolling. Remember that if you can believe it, you can receive it.

The Word is Power

The Bible says, "As the Father has life, the Son has life." We have been taught all our lives that there is but one ultimate life force, mind, and spirit. This force may be called by many names by many religions under many faiths; nonetheless, there is but one. This energy is a part of our lives, and it dwells in mankind and all living creatures. It is manifested through us as we believe in it.

When we speak our thoughts, we speak life-affirming words. We cannot do any of this alone. Without the connection of the energy source, we are without power. Without the Word of God—or a sense of connection to him—we cannot manifest anything from anywhere. We become powerless, and our words do not bear fruit. Our words only have power when they are one with the infinite power.

We are completely surrounded by a spirit of consciousness and a universal thought that computes into law. Through the combination of the two, everything that was made is made. "In the beginning was the Word and the Word was with God and the Word was God." –John 1:1

The Holy Scripture states, "All things were made by him and without him nothing was made that were made. In him was life and the life was the light of men. And the light shined in the darkness and the darkness comprehended it not." John 1:3-5

Words give form to the unformed. The greater the thought process of the conscious mind, the more power punch the words have. Words without connection have no power—and a connection without words will never generate the necessary frequency of vibrational energy to manifest desires. The law of the universe states that there must be a combination of the two in order for man to purposely manifest anything into reality.

We are Avatars on Earth

Scripture says, "This world is not our home." We must be guests on a planet where everything appears to be physical. We are individuals living in a universe of law and order. This universal law teaches us cause and effect. At home, our experiences would be very different. There would be no physical—only spiritual. The spiritual is infinite life—where we call home. There would be no negative—only positive, life-affirming energy. Holy Scriptures were passed down through the ages, written by cultures whose thinking and thoughts were reaching inward as well as outward toward an infinite reality. There is but one mind in the universe and that mind exists in everything and everywhere. All thoughts lead to this truth, and all truths lead to an eternal home with the infinite one.

Scripture teaches us that no man can go to heaven unless he came from heaven—and that he cannot go to or come from heaven unless he is already there. It must be clear that we are still connected with the infinite one—just as we were in the beginning before time. Energy does not know time; it only knows continuation to infinity. Only that which was born in heaven can return to heaven. After all, it is like we became unconscious of home yesterday.

We must be born of the spirit in order to be conscious of the infinite one or Supreme Being. We call it enlightenment or awakening. We cannot be born of the spirit unless we do the will of the spirit. The will of the spirit is truth, love, forgiveness, peace compassion, strength, and a sound mind. All of this allows us to have a consciousness with our God. It establishes an inner sense of reality. In this reality, there is no doubt but the strong faith of the invisible.

Somewhere down the path of life, we will one day awake to the fact that we co-create our own heaven and hell. We all have been given the power to manifest our reality. We all live in spirit, utilizing thoughts without true knowledge of their use. Mankind has the gift through words or thoughts, but few utilize it or recognize it.

In a Trance?

One of the greatest authorities of all has planted the idea in our minds that an evil place after this life does not exist. It has put mankind in a somewhat hypnotic state. I believe that most of mankind is walking around in this hypnotic state. They think and believe whatever they are taught to believe. Their beliefs are very shallow and do not dig down to the roots of any concept.

Metaphysical concepts are as far from their understanding as the idea of walking on water or healing the sick. We must snap out of the trance and resist the hypnotic power that has built up authority in our lives. If we can remember, we co-create what we see and feel. Why put another authority over our lives? Are we so in need of a leader because of our own weaknesses? We should consider leaving this outside authority to less evolved people and set our thoughts on the idea of freedom. I am referring to a freedom to proclaim oneness with the infinite one and dare to stand on the true metaphysical principals and laws of the universe.

Through our beliefs and daily living practices, we are co-creating a reality for ourselves that will produce what we believe in. This universal law of manifestation was set in place long before we were brought into physical being. Through our thoughts, we create our heaven, our hell, and our present reality. If our affirmations are a vibrational match, we create. We do not have to believe that we create—the law works whether we believe it or not. The infinite one can do anything for us through us. We must first believe and let him into our reality. Scripture says, "Behold I stand at the door and knock." The world is there for our taking—if only we let Him in.

It is clear that positive energy and negative energy cannot occupy the same space. It is believed that upon death of the physical body, the spirit or soul will leave the body and cross the veil of life that leads to home on the other side. An evil person or murderer has not evolved enough to enter the bright light of the other side. I believe these persons go to their own hell. They go to a place to work on getting it right before recycling the soul. I believe that this place is what one would call hell. It may not be the biblical hell that we have been taught all our lives with fire, brimstone, and a lake of fire that will burn into eternity, but it is a true hell.

The best thing to remember is that we, as eternal energy, have a chance to get it right through reincarnation until the rapture. I do believe that when the rapture comes, it is "game over." Most religions—with the exception of Christianity—believe in reincarnation. In the beginning,

Christians believed in reincarnation. It was not until the First Council of Nicaea and the Chalcedon in AD 451 that enlightenment and the causes for future teachings of incarnation or rebirth were deleted from Christian doctrine. I'm guessing that during this period, the fathers of the Christian movement needed more control over the people. We can speculate about why it was removed, but no one really knows why. We only know that the prophets were inspired by the Holy Spirit to write the Bible. Nothing was to be added or taken away. We know that man has added and taken away so much from the Bible.

How Can I Find a Healer?

An individual who has been blessed with the gift of healing knows that the healing work takes place within the subconscious mind. A healer reaches inside to touch the soul of the ill person. It must be understood that the healing words are in "your own mouth," and there alone can they be spoken in truth. There is no doubt from the healer of the words that he or she speaks. People do not understand this manner of healing. They are waiting for lightning to strike, earthquakes to tremble, or some other grand sign to show a miraculous, healing event.

If we have embraced the love of the infinite one in our lives and truly understand his connection to us, we possess the power to heal. At one time or another, we will be called upon to help a distressed person, comfort them in sorrow, pray for a disease to cease, or do other metaphysical works of healing. During this time of healing others, we are also healing ourselves. All healing works of man take place within himself. Some healing works are meant to take place with healing, and others are meant for comfort due to the manifestation of the word.

Man has no power without the Supreme Being that has connected life with darkness. Therefore, words of healing should be said with absolute faith. The word can establish the law of life unto any person. It is the person's job to believe and pray continuously to place the healing words into their vibration. Remembering who we are as eternal beings restores our health. The power is already waiting within us—we need only remember it. We are only priming others with faith in the unseen realm of power.

One cannot claim to be healed, and then turn around and confess that they are sick. It is important to live and act as though you have been healed already—in that case, you have.

God has no respect for time. If it is meant that you are to be healed, you have already been healed from the beginning of time. The infinite one is just waiting for us to realize that we do not have to go through what we are going through. We just have to reach out and claim what he has done for us in advance. He is waiting for us to evolve to a certain point in time where we can claim our healing. The healing is actually waiting on us. Some illnesses are meant to be used as a way home; others are never meant to be. Some illnesses are manifestations of our words.

I believe that it is necessary to give you a brief summary of my miraculous healing. I hesitate to bring up painful thoughts of despair, desperation, isolation, pain, and dependence on over-the-counter medications and prescriptions. This would mean bringing something negative back into my vibration—if only for a short time.

My journey started long before I knew that I was going to experience severe health problems. I believe that an accumulation of negative people, conversations, food, relationships, work, and an aging body brought on this alleged sickness. I refused to give the energy any power; therefore, it is not real to me. At the tender age of forty-two, I crawled to the bathroom on my knees. I could not hold my head up to speak—let alone to eat. My grandmother cared for me daily. My body was in severe pain all day and all night. I could find no relief in medicine or therapy. I was diagnosed with severe arthritis of the spine, chronic fatigue, severe fibromyalgia, and manic depression. I used a walker to get around the house. When I went to the store, I used a cane and rode an electric shopping cart. My pain was unbearable. The doctors said it would get worse over time. My marriage was falling apart, and my children desperately needed their mother.

I went to the ministers and pastors of my church. They offered me prayer and told me that I was healed. With all respect, I should have been healed, but—deep in my mind—I did not believe I was healed. I would say I was healed—but also confess that I was sick and in pain. I did not know how to release my burden.

I did not know that the power to be healed was right there inside of me. I kept looking for a big event to take place. I was looking for instant gratification or euphoria. I wanted to throw down my cane or walker, run out of the house, and scream about how great I felt. I didn't realize that I was already healed. I just needed to accept that which was already given to me by God. God knew this day was coming long before I was born or even thought of. I just needed to wake up to the fact that God should come first in my life. If I put the kingdom of God before all things, everything else would be added unto me. I had to learn to make time for him. I always had time for my career and family, but I put God's work last. When I became ill, I started putting God first. I still did not know how to tap into this energy of healing, love, forgiving, prosperity, abundance, generosity, peace of mind, and gratitude and honor for him.

I spent years withdrawn into myself, not seeking, asking, or wanting to continue a life so full of pain. My strength was found in my children. They gave me the courage to continue with faith that there was help—and I was not destined to live a life of pain and agony.

When my cousin Eva came to visit, I pulled away from personal visits. I made them short and to the point. I always had to lie down from to the pain. I never stayed on my feet more than a few hours a day. I always had an excuse to escape the company of others. Yet, when I told my cousin about my agony, she said, "I think I can help you."

She started to work with me by giving me different books written by spiritual ministers that worked through the new thought type of doctrine. She also gave me literature on psychics and mediums. As I began to read, I intuitively felt the spirit within.

When I began to speak the words of healing, the false belief of doubt disappeared. The words destroyed any false sense of a material life that I had been holding onto. The words helped me realize that everything within me is an expression of the most perfect infinite one that also dwells in me.

When I became sure of myself and my beliefs, I began to heal. Doubt was gone. I had been visited by God and his angels. I even saw the angels. When I asked for confirmation of my thoughts, the spirit provided it without hesitation. I was intuitively guided by my spiritual guides in how to eat healthily, how to use the doctor's medicine in conjunction with the healing spirit, and how to release the negativity in my life and focus on the positive. I have learned that if you can believe it, you can receive it—in all things.

When you are as sure of your beliefs as you are in yourself, you will not only heal yourself, but you will have the ability through the infinite one to heal others as well. When you are as sure as the air you breathe that an ill person is healed after you speak the true words, there is no doubt that they are healed. This is not what I call faith healing. This is true healing from a power within the self. The ill person must also be a believer. One major rule to remember is that all vibrations must match in order to manifest. If all vibrations match, you need only speak the words from your own mouth. A healer's work takes place within the self first. If your patient does not believe that they are healed, it is not your fault. You will have done all that you can do through the power of the infinite one.

When the ministers, pastors, and evangelists were trying to heal me, I wondered what was wrong with them. Were they false in their spirits? I took no responsibility for not being healed. I did not know that there was something else I needed to do besides going to church and saying a prayer or two. I had to learn that God was—and is—a lot deeper than that. I found a healer—right there inside of me.

The same power that made me sick also healed me. The truth is that there is but one subjective mind in the universe. This subjective mind can be impressed upon by any thought. The mind is totally creative in all things. The spirit within man is the infinite one—and we know that the infinite one is creative at all times in everything that is asked. You must remember that we are dealing with a universal principle or a mental law.

In *Science of the Mind,* Ernest Homes said, "Spiritual mind healing is a result of the constructive use of mental law. Since we are thinking beings and cannot stop thinking, and since creative mind receives our thoughts and cannot stop creating, it must always be creating something for us. What it will make depends wholly upon what we are thinking, and what we shall attract will depend upon that on which our thoughts dwell." It is through the power of attraction this law works for us.

If we were only dealing with the power of a thought, we could not heal anyone or anything. We are dealing with a universal principal. *In Spiritual Liberation,* Michael Bernard Beckwith said, "We should not set any limits to what the infinite one can do." This law has been put in place for our purpose—for our needs, for our comforts, and for our choices.

If I think that I am sick, the universe will produce that thought. If I dwell on healing and perfect wellness, the universe will produce just that thought. Look at how wonderful this law is and how it works for us.

"Most of us attract by default. We just think that we don't have any control over it. Our thoughts and feelings are on autopilot, and so everything is brought to us by default."

—**Bob Doyle**

A SHIFT IN REALITY

I affirm that I am well and am healed.
I am prosperous.
I am filled with gratitude.
I am one with the infinite one.
I am at peace with life.

Through mental ability, man has created destruction, illness, dreams, technology, healing, prosperity, and anything that the mind can conceive. Through ignorance, we have misused the power of thought. The infinite one provides us with everything we could possibly need or want.

All we have to do is think about it and ask for it in our minds. Thoughts have the power to create. Charles Fillmore said, "We must choose what thoughts we are going to lose in the mind and what thoughts we are going to bind, for they will come into manifestation in our affairs."

Man has a power within that can overcome all obstacles in his life. He has the power to heal himself and others, create prosperity, destroy nations, and discover the secrets of physical life. He has the power to create physical life and destroy all that is different than himself. I have been blessed with a vision that shows a shift in our reality. The vision shows us developing and accepting our spiritual guidance from our Supreme Being. I see a new people—full of vigor, life, and intuitive guidance. They have faith in the same word—but a new vision. I can clearly see an evolved people.

There is talk among mediums, psychics, and mystics of a planetary shift in consciousness. This shift should allow people to accept one another as they are with the infinite one. God has given us many gifts: visions, prophecies, songs, musical instruments, psychic abilities, preaching, dreaming, speaking in tongues, and interpreting tongues. This shift in our reality can only bring positive enlightenment into our current evolutionary state. We are all constantly evolving into the best we can possibly be in a spiritual and physical awakening.

A shift in our reality brings about the power of thought. The power of thought brings about spiritual mind healing, the active mind within one mind, and how we set our own limitations through thought and understanding. The Bible says, "As a man thinketh in his heart, so is he."

In *Science of the Mind,* Ernest Homes stated, "In the field of mental and physical healing, this area is looked upon by man as obscure and imperfectly understood, because the scientific study of the mind is still in its infancy stages. It is a fact that the misuse of mental and spiritual laws are at the root of many depressed conditions, as incidents in the physical life stand out clear and sharp."

If I can believe it, I can achieve it. If I can think it, I can create it. Over the ages, mystics and metaphysicians have realized that all causation is from within. This shift in reality or consciousness has opened the minds of many nonbelievers, creating a shift in the world in reference to the universal law of thought.

Self-Defeating Behavior

I often talk to my children about self-defeating behaviors that can alter their lives forever—whether it is positive or negative reinforcers. As mentioned earlier, we are cocreators of our destiny and life experiences. When we release that which is negative in nature, we can make room within our minds in order to evolve into our next dimension as a living being. This evolutionary state is in constant progress. We are forever growing spiritually and physically.

Our minds are forever expanding in truth and technology. When I speak of truth, I am only talking about the one eternal truth that is constantly shifting our consciousness and bringing our spirit into a full circle of reality. Our self-defeating behavior limits our manifestation of prosperity, perfect health, happiness, and all our inherited rights.

I often lecture two of my children specifically about behavior. I explain how they are creating the very thing that they do not want by thinking about it, dwelling on it, and saying they do not want it. They have, in reality, created the very thing that they do not want. When you think it, you place it into your vibration. The law of the universe does not know the words "no" or "do not." It only knows "give." For instance, my teenager tells me that she wants the latest iPod. I tell her it is okay, but she will have to earn it. To keep it, her behavior must be that which is desired in our home. If she breaks the rules, she may get her luxury item confiscated for any number of days or weeks. She agrees to the conditions, but proceeds to do the very thing that she has been warned about. Constantly doing things that hurt is self-defeating behavior. Every time things are going in the direction that she wants them to go, unconsciously the conditioned self steps in and defeats all positive behavior toward her desired goal.

Let's take a different approach to understanding self-defeating behavior. As we know, the infinite one gave us the power to heal our lives. In *Hidden Powers of the Bible,* Ernest Home said, "We must first clarify our own vision, then we shall become as lights lighting the way for others."

Jesus said to the faithful centurion, "Go thy way; and as thou has believed, so be it done unto thee."

We cannot say one thing and believe another; this behavior is totally self-defeating.

The Mental State of Receptiveness

We must train our minds to listen to that inner voice of truth from within. We are inspired with love, a sound mind, and strength. There is an intuitive voice that speaks to all people at all times. Some of us may hear this voice during quiet times and moments of solitude; others may hear this voice at any given moment. This voice or intuitive feeling is our higher consciousness. The more successful we are in life, health, wealth, happiness, sound mind, endurance, and strength, the more we can express our true selves through the God Within. If we are not mentally ready to perceive what is born of the spirit, how can we receive what is offered by spirit?

Our mental state cannot be receptive if we do not recognize that we are born of the spirit. We cannot be born of the spirit unless we do the will of the spirit; the will of the spirit is light over darkness, good over evil, mercy, justice, truth compassion, love, sound mind, and overall goodness and strength with our higher consciousness. There is a higher consciousness in a union with the infinite one.

Christ said, "Thou must be born again." We must be born of the spirit—for that which is born of spirit is spirit. This new birth comes not by our observation or loud proclamation but by an inner truth and sense of what is actually real. Christ is referring to the heavenly birth of knowledge, truth, and spirit. Our concentration in life must be complete with purpose. In making this journey, you must have a purpose-driven life.

The Bible states, "Unless a man be born again, he cannot see the kingdom of God."

What Shifts Our Reality?

Eternal energy within self connects with the infinite one and intuitively guides our every thought and action. We see the confirmation of truth within our lives daily. For some of us, it is through affirmations and confirmations of self. For others, the still voice of guidance and love penetrates every fiber of our existence.

We all have two voices that always talk within us. The one true voice says, "I do not author fear, but love, strength, and a sound mind. I am the way and the light. Do not be afraid; your visions your intuitive feelings are true. As you walk in spirit toward this tunnel of light, you will find the other half of self and discover that this tunnel opens within your own mind. You will discover a higher consciousness within self."

That second voice is saying that you are following an illusion. What the religious leaders and scholars are preaching is not real. Make yourself happy and live to the fullest for self. This is a voice of despair and darkness. Without a choice within the heart of man, there can be no truth—only dominion.

Mystics through the ages have been professing that thought is man's only barrier between his higher consciousness and self. Through the evolution of man's mind and technology, more people are beginning to realize the eternal energy that is omnipresent within the universe of life.

In *Spiritual Liberation,* Michael Bernard Beckwith said, "A state of being aware that you are aware. It is a realization that you are the watcher, the witness within you. When you consciously realize that you are the observer, it is then you can become free from manmade labels. Such as ethnicity labels gender identity labels, religious labels, political labels, and so forth."

All of these must be set aside in order for a true shift in our reality to take place within each of us. Our consciousness is the fundamental building block of our reality. If we as a people continue to raise our consciousness—thus sustaining and formulating our pure divine nature through the universal law—we can shift the universal reality into a place that could be perceived as heaven.

Heaven? The Bible states, "No man hath ascended up to heaven, but he that came down from heaven, even the Son of man which is in heaven."

Christ is one of the greatest mystics of all. His words are clear without any hidden meaning but are difficult for the un-evolved man to understand. He states that no man can go to heaven unless he came from heaven and that he cannot go or come from this place called heaven unless he is already there. This statement tells us that heaven is not a place, but a state of consciousness. The return must also be recognized that heaven is already within. It is believed through biblical interpretation that the Son of man, who is also the son of the infinite one, is already in heaven and knows it not. Man must understand the life principles to be spiritual and not in a material sense in order to completely shift the universal consciousness into a state of heaven.

Michael Bernard Beckwith says, "As you unleash your inner self to reach the unreachable star, live the impossible dream, you allow possibility to take root in your consciousness; your agreements with mediocrity will begin to dissolve and you will enter the evolutionary process of becoming creatively maladjusted."

A universal maladjustment could only mean a shift in the world's reality. I have focused my thoughts and purpose on this shift in reality. It is here most will find heaven.

What is the Other Side?

Let's not confuse heaven with the other side. I believe these to be two separate places and ideologies. Psychics will tell you that there is truly another side to our reality. Mystics will tell you that this other side only exists in our minds—and we presently dwell within it. Hindus and Buddhists will tell you that neither exists—there is only birth, suffering, death, and rebirth until total absorption with Brahman. The Muslims and the average Christian will tell you of only a separate heaven or hell that awaits all. You must remember that you create your reality. Our heaven or our hell—and all that exists within ourselves—await us in the afterlife. There is no wrong or right answer to the afterlife. Universal law is set in place to give us what we think of. Our faith, thoughts, and beliefs are constantly in motion, creating for us. If we are coming from a dark side, we are going to a dark side. If we are coming from a light side, we are going to the light.

If we believe in nothing, we are going to nothing. Our vibration in life must be a match. You cannot ask for something and believe in the absence of it.

"You attract to you the predominant thoughts that you're holding in your awareness, whether those thoughts are conscious or unconscious."

—Michael Bernard Beckwith

CONSCIOUS THOUGHT

I affirm that my mind, body, and spirit are healed.
I affirm that everything I need is within me.
I affirm that I am the co-creator of my experiences.
I affirm that I am prosperous in all things.

In this chapter, I want to remind you that God is not a person, but a presence personified in us. The Holy Spirit is not a being but an energy within the atmosphere, which is the presence of "I Am." This energy is eternal and the most powerful in the universe. This energy is personified in us or connected to us as an unborn child to its mother. All is one—and one is all.

In *Science of the Mind,* Ernest Holmes said, "We must bring into our experience which we have not experienced before; bringing it in as the result of conscious thought; and unless it is possible to do this, our whole science is a mistake and a delusion. Unless there is a divine principle universal soul or subjectivity, or medium, which, of itself—without any help or assistance—can produce things, and will, then there is nothing in any religious or metaphysical teaching."

Thought

Here I want to reiterate that our thoughts become the things thought of. What we have in life and how we live our lives is the result of a man's thought. Our mindset has everything to do with our health, prosperity, peace, happiness, and success. What we possess, how we live our lives, and the condition of our lives are the result of subjective thought.

I believe that thoughts are things. I believe this because our thoughts are manifested into forms. The thought process is part of the universal law. I meditate daily and acknowledge and value the unseen world as alive and real. This is all part of thought. What you place your values on in your life will grow and prosper in your life. Believe me—it is that simple.

There are as many different ways of accessing the invisible or spiritual world as there are traditions. History has demonstrated that each has its own unique offering to the metaphysical balance within the universe: meditation, prayer, martial arts, and dance, religious ministering, being one with nature, and so on. We all need to first find what connects our minds to that ultimate source of energy or that greater sense of life that the mystics call the infinite one.

The Healer

I believe that some of us are confused by thought and healing. We believe that energy heals us. I do not believe that energy itself is what heals. I believe that energy brings forth information and helps us remember—and that's what heals us. Before we became avatars, what were we? Before we became part of this human experience, what were we?

The answer to this is clear—we were with and part of him. In him, there is no disease or imperfection; there is only perfection and abundanceJesus the Christ made all of this very clear in the Holy Bible. The Holy Bible is not the only inspired holy book written through inspiration of the Holy Spirit. It's just the one that I am using to reference from at this time; to find the healer within, we must invest in what we do not know. Most people only invest in what they know or think they know. It is difficult to alter old ground in religious traditions or beliefs. You may find it easier to chop a redwood tree down with only an ax.

My job is to help you open up to what you do not know but think that you know and what you cannot see but ultimately feel in your spiritual guidance system. To help you get past all these ingrained fear-based ideologies and misconceptions of the truth. To find the healer, we must access the unseen world of spirit. When it comes to matters that peer into the vastness of life and being, we can be pretty sure that what we think we know, we have a lot more to learn on the subject. I do know that 99 percent of the unseen world is reality, but we place 99 percent of our undivided attention upon the seen world. That pathway to healing a person accesses the unseen world. When we access the unseen, we access the eternal energy of the ultimate energy source.

You can help yourself as well as others access it by being comfortable, familiar, and valuing, honoring, and knowing the spirit for yourself. No matter how much we think that we know or understand the laws and the workings of the human soul and the spirit and all the unseen realms, we are really only touching on the edge of this knowledge. Some have more knowledge than others—and some have more of a connection than others—but all have some. When we influence the unseen world through thought, we influence the seen world.

Should I Take Prescription Medication?

My advice would be to take your prescribed medications. The infinite one made doctors and all the herbs and medicines available to you. Some illnesses are presented in order to edify his name and glory. Basically, all illnesses are illusions in themselves. However, they are as real as real can get to mankind. What I would have to say concerning this subject is to let the doctors treat the illness—and let the metaphysicians treat the spirit. After all, we must focus on the spirit in order to heal the physical body. The healing is already within. It is the truth that actually heals the physical body. A metaphysician has no power alone. God within possess the power. Without this energy source, all that is could not possibly be all that life is. They would be merely words and void of all consciousness and life.

In the Holy Bible, the Archangel Raphael collected fish parts to place on Tobit's eyes. He knew that this concoction would be useful in healing and restoring Tobit's sight. Again, let the doctors treat the physical body and let the metaphysician treat the spirit. If the spirit can be healed or even touched, the body can only follow the lead and be healed.

The statements that are made here are not to be considered dogmatic. The mind of man must realize that all power is given unto him. He must believe that his core is spiritual and that his physical body is only a shell or house for the spirit. We must think of our entire being as a true spiritual being searching for a connecting outlet in the physical man. We must enter a state of knowing that the mind is—everything that can be thought. Without faith in this concept, we cannot grow. Our evolutionary growth becomes stagnated and bound without the words. If we can study to show ourselves approved in the words and have the faith of a mustard seed, the Holy Bible says, "All things will be added unto us."

What is Faith?

Faith is the belief in a substance that cannot be seen but knowingly exists. It is a mental exercise that is completely positive in nature and constantly creating. Faith is a belief in the invisible law that directly responds to man.

Jesus said, "Thy faith has made thee whole." Therefore, faith is an action word, which is a verb in the English language. It is always in motion, creating, and manifesting through thought. "It is the substance of things hoped for and the evidence of things not seen."

In the process of helping self though this life, one truly must have faith. Faith in what? The answer to this question is in whatever you believe in or do not believe in.

While working on my dissertation in seminary school, my research and qualitative study was on comparative religion—in conflict, life after death, and reincarnation. I discovered that we as a people are all connected through the spirit. We are connected intuitively and spiritually.

In *In the Spirit,* Susan L. Taylor said, "It is your positive or negative faith which is creating your future ... faith is potent stuff. It's a generator. What we believe is the starting point of what we experience."

Take your doctor-prescribed medication—and call the metaphysician for a dose of spiritual healing. It all works on its own level, just as water seeks its own level. What is good for the spirit is good for the spirit and what is good for the physical body is good for the physical body. Remember, the metaphysician works on a spiritual level, affecting the spiritual and physical man. The physical doctor works on a physical level, affecting only what our spirit will allow to be affected physically.

"What most people don't understand is that a thought has a frequency. We can measure a thought ... Our job as humans is to hold on to the thoughts of what we want, make it absolutely clear in our minds what we want, and from that we start to invoke one of the greatest laws in the universe, and that's the law of attraction. You become what you think about most, but you also attract what you think about most."

—**John Assaraf**

THE WORD: RISEN FROM THE DEAD

I affirm that I know only perfection in him.
I affirm that I am free to live a joyous,
healthy, prosperous life.
I affirm that the universal law is put in place for my needs.
I affirm that it is my birthright to walk
with the infinite one forever.
I affirm that death is only an illusion
and life is eternal in spirit.

I would like to discuss the Word. What is the Word? Why do I need to know or understand the Word? Look around you—what do you see, hear, or feel? Whatever it is, it began with a word or the Word. Nothing in this universe could be created without a thought or something touched by an energy that carried within it intelligence which created infinite spirit. It created itself from self. There was nothing that it could create itself from other than self.

One of the most profound statements in the Bible states, "In the beginning was the Word, and the Word was with God and the Word was God. In him was life and the life was the light of men. And the light shineth in the darkness and the darkness comprehended it not."

What are we supposed to comprehend? We are supposed to comprehend the Word. The Word is the infinite energy source, our beginning, and our end.

We are talking about an infinite intelligent energy source that created all from self. According to St. John, "All things were made by him and without him was not anything made that was made."

The Word was crucified in the flesh but rose on the third day in the spirit. Yes, the flesh was said to get up and walk again and talk. The Word showed a disciple named Thomas the nail holes in his hand to prove who he was. Yet only the spirit went home to sit at the right hand of the I Am. The Word and the Father are one—just as the Father and we are one. Yes, I said it: Jesus was not the only son of God (Infinite). We are also sons and daughters of the infinite source of life.

It is the quickening of the spirit within us that leaves us standing on the edge of a new thought. Just as the Word spoke to the religious leaders, disciples, priests, and gurus in the early days of our religious quest, it speaks to us today in the quietness and stillness of our minds.

When the Infinite one rose from the dead in three days and ascended into the heavens, he didn't stop revealing to his people or abandon his people. He speaks to us in dreams and visions. He speaks to us intuitively—and sometimes he just speaks out loud.

The Voice I Heard

In June 1987, I was driving along a busy street in Lansing, Michigan. My son Christopher was strapped into his car seat in the back. Most of the time, I drive in silence since it gives me time to reflect, hear, and focus on what's going on around me.

My little white sports car hummed along in perfect working condition. I was in somewhat of a hurry, but I do not remember why. I just hated busy traffic and could not wait to get onto a much calmer street. As I approached the intersection of an equally busy street, the light turned green. *Great*, I thought.

When I proceeded through the intersection, a clear voice said, "Terry, stop."

I immediately stopped my vehicle in the middle of the intersection with the green light in front of me. As I stopped, a huge old late model Cadillac whooshed by me so fast it caused my little car to sway. All the other vehicles had already stopped behind and to the side of me.

I said, "Thank you, Jesus. I am so glad that I listened in a time that was unusual as far as the request was concerned."

That car would have caused a fatality if it had hit anyone. I was sitting in the middle of the intersection with my son in the back seat, wondering what had happened. Even though there have been many different incidents throughout the years where the voice of spirit was clear and either warning, protecting, or guiding, none has been as profound as the Lansing incident.

In Visions, Dreams, and Forms

As I evolved spiritually over the years, I have learned to become aware of spirit. The presence of the Word or spirit or whatever name you give to your higher consciousness is as real and forthcoming as any physical form. The Holy Spirit may come in a vision or a dream, revealing information for your life journey. It may come just to make its presence known to you.

As I look back over my life, I remember experiencing the actual vision of forms which are really spirits. Over the years, I have had many encounters.

When my husband Herschel passed away, I moved to Cascade Township, Michigan. A few years had passed since we had moved to the area. Christopher was about eleven years old and Aaron was around five. I had been experiencing a form for a few years before making it known to my family. I did not understand spirit or have an open connection with the other side. Everything that I saw and did not understand was based on fear. This fear was based on religious ideologies taught throughout my life.

The forms sometimes frightened me. They frightened me because I did not understand them. They frightened me because I had been taught early on to fear them. I remember chanting words that I was told to chant or speak if spirits were seen in my home. Looking back over those days, I surely do have some regrets. I understand now that the connection was only made out of love. Everything that spirit does is out of love.

Christopher said, "Mom, I keep seeing Herschel sitting over there in that big white chair."

I was shocked because I thought I was the only person that could see him in that chair. Herschel was my deceased husband. There was another entity that would walk past my bedroom door every evening. This would happen five or six times a week—sometimes multiple times in one evening. I did not recognize the form, and there was no concern other than what it was and what it wanted.

One of the most recent sightings was at our church in Haines City, Florida, at the eight o'clock service. Pastor Babers was well into his sermon when I saw with my third eye that there was a form in the pulpit with him. The angelic form was moving about the pulpit as though it was familiar with it. I closed my eyes to see if it would disappear, but it didn't. I wondered if I was becoming delusional.

Throughout the service, I watched the angelic form move around the pulpit. My daughter had told me and the pastor several months earlier that she had seen an angel in the pulpit while he was giving his sermon.

As we drove home, my daughter said, "Mom, I want you to know that I saw another angel in the pulpit with pastor today."

I looked at her in astonishment and said, "Aaron, me too."

We exchanged notes on what we had seen. It is evident that my daughter is highly clairvoyant. If only I can get her to work with her gift instead of just living with it. Her gifts in the spirit always amaze me.

What Does Spirit Want?

According to some very famous psychic mediums such as Sylvia Brown, James Van Praagh, and John Edward, all that spirits want to do is to make contact with us in order to show us that life exists after death. They do this out of love. They want to show us that they are all right and that there is nothing to fear. The contact that they make is made out of love.

Word is alive and well even in this present day. He is still giving revelations, gifts, visions, prophecies, life, protection, and prosperity. We can train our minds through meditation and prayer to become more sensitive to the presence of spirits and what is trying to be shared by them.

"The spiritual substance from which comes all visible wealth is never depleted. It is right with you all the time and responds to your faith in it and your demands on it."

—**Charles Fillmore (1854–1948)**

HEALING WITH CRYSTALS AND THE CHAKRAS

I affirm that the earth is a living, evolving entity.
I affirm that the earth has force fields of subtle energies.
I affirm that we are all connected to all that is or ever was.

Through my studies and life experience, I have learned that earth is living, breathing, and constantly evolving—just as we are. It has a force field of energies—just like all living creatures. It possesses veins, arteries, and various minerals. There is an energy center that receives and transmits from the beginning to the end of space and time. Crystals are mineral transmitters and receivers of cosmic energy that are buried deep within the earth.

During the time of the pharaohs, crystals and many other gemstones were used to heal and provide needed amplification to the appropriate chakra center on the human body. Healers would place the appropriate crystal on the specific chakra area and meditate upon it or pray to the Holy Spirit to initiate energy into healing.

Chakra System

Each chakra area has a specific color. The chakra system consists of seven areas of the body. The first chakra—the base or root chakra—is located at the base of the spine. The color of this chakra is perceived as red. It is the energy center through which a person would experience "flight or fight." It governs the kidneys and the spinal column.

The second chakra, located right below the navel, is the chakra center for creativity. It is usually called the sacral chakra. It governs sex and reproduction and is perceived as orange.

The third chakra is located in the solar plexus. It is below the ribcage but above the navel. It is perceived to be yellow and governs the nervous system, liver, spleen, stomach, and gall bladder. The fourth chakra is the heart chakra. This chakra governs the heart, blood, and circulatory system. This is the center in which we feel love. Its color is perceived as green. The fifth chakra, the throat chakra, is located at the base of the throat. It governs the lungs, vocal cords, bronchial system, and metabolism. It is the center of our communication. It is perceived as blue.

The sixth chakra or trine is located in the center of the forehead. It is known as the third eye. It governs the brain, nervous system, ears, nose, and the left eye. This is one of our centers that connect us with our spiritual nature. Its color is perceived as indigo. The seventh or crown chakra is located at the top of the head. It governs the upper brain and right eye. Through this chakra or trine, one may ultimately reach the feeling of integration with the infinite source. Its color is perceived as violet.

There are many healing methods. The process of working with the body and aligning it, mind, body, and spirit, through meditation and visualization with the aid of crystals or prayer makes you a healer in your own right. Remember that it is not the physical you that does the healing. It is the power of God within you. By calming your mind and allowing the intervention of spirit to take control, you become an awakened being, fully recognizing that you are spiritual and functioning on not only a spiritual level but a level that affects the mind and body as well.

The crystals are only carrying the blessed information through vibrations. Everything in the universe has a vibration. It is known through scientific discovery that even the color of light is expressed in various vibrations, depending on the individual color. Each color of the chakra system resonates to its own level of vibration—as well as its corresponding level of consciousness.

Gemstone Elixirs or Crystal Essence and Gem Water

I prefer to make and ingest gemstone elixirs. It is also referred to as gem essence or gem water. I make these elixirs by placing the gemstone in purified or kangen water. I place the water and the stones in the sunlight. I believe that the energetic signature of a crystal can be imprinted on the molecules of water. By doing this, you can introduce the healing properties of a crystal to the body directly. Mystics believe that essence water enables the body to balance itself on its own time.

Making gem water is very simple. Place a cleansed crystal or gemstone in a glass or pitcher. Fill with kangen water or spring water. Cover and leave outside overnight. In the morning, remove the stones and sip on the water throughout the day. The water should keep in the refrigerator for a few days.

To make gem essence water, you need to leave it out in the sunlight for two to three hours. At that time, add equal parts of 80-proof vodka to the charged water. The alcohol acts as a preservative. Pour a small amount of the water into a small bottle with a dropper.

Since the gem essence is very strong, only use two or three drops at a time. It can be placed on the tongue, rubbed on the chakra area, or placed on the pulse points within the body. It can even be added to bath water. Never use more than two or three drops at one time due to the potency.

There are many therapies with the use of crystals that can be used for healing the body. I suggest that you invest in a book on crystal healing. The amount of information is so vast that it could totally absorb the information that I am giving you.

The Vibration of Colors

Each chakra has its own keynote. For example, if the vibration of the first chakra, which is the root chakra, could be heard, it would resonate the note of C. The second chakra would resonate the note of D, and so on up the scale.

When I meditate on a chakra color, I chant the sound "Om" by humming the note that each color would correspond with. "Om" is said to be the most audible word or sound duplicating the vibration of the infinite energy within us and on the other side. It is such a powerful word.

It has been used for many eons to place harmony in healing. This chant can place you in a deeper state of consciousness during meditation.

Something about Seven

Mystics say that there are seven levels of consciousness: physical, etheric, emotional, mental, astral, spiritual, and soul. There are seven colors in the rainbow. There are seven energy centers in the body. There are seven colors that correspond to the seven energy centers. There are seven notes on a music scale. If we could hear color in a musical language, the notes would be higher than audible sound.

Sound Meditation

Sound has a profound effect on healing. I have used sound as a healing tool for years. Sometimes you must listen to the sound beyond the silence. Harsh noises drive me insane. High pitches or the sound of bickering temperamentally disturb me. The sounds that technology has created are unnatural. The progress of society has created noise that pollutes the air. To escape this sound pollution and hustle and bustle of people, I moved to a rural area. The simple things bring balance to my life, mind, and spirit.

As a metaphysician, I recommend recording natural sounds and saving them for your time of meditation. Some people like the sound of trucks, cars, trains, and sirens. They have been conditioned to such plastic pollutants in the air that they cannot live without them. Then they wonder why they are so stressed out and uptight about everything and anything. They can't figure out why they have the physical diseases of the body and mind. These unnatural sounds bring an unnatural balance to the body.

They change our vibration within our energy centers. Changes to our natural vibrations alter our chemical makeup. They cause the body to excrete different chemicals into our bloodstream. Our physical bodies react to what is going on around us. Any medical doctor will tell you that our bodies excrete certain hormones and chemicals based upon our reaction to our environment. This is a good thing if we are in the flight-or-fight stages. At other times, it wears on our hearts, livers, endocrine glands, and other major organs.

Subconsciously, we carry around high stress in our bodies. We are in search of something but do not know what. We go to massage therapists, hot tubs, or saunas. We are looking for a peaceful, quiet place that can allow us to enter into the mind of self. My advice is to start with the sounds around you. Subconsciously, they are being grounded into your being daily.

When we listen to music that we think is beautiful, the oscillation of the music's vibration touches our innermost parts. This, in turn, affects a balance that improves our natural circulation, metabolism, and endocrine glands. Sound is a universal language. In all of nature, sound helps all to vibrate as one. If the sound is not compatible, it causes distortion in the cells or tissues of the living matter.

"If you have a disease, and you are focusing on it, and you're talking to people about it, you're going to create more diseased cells. See yourself living in a perfectly healthy body. Let the doctor look after the disease."

—**Bob Proctor**

RENEWING OF YOUR MIND INTO A NEW BIRTH

I affirm that my mind has been renewed.
I affirm that I am healed in his presence.
I affirm that the Word is my strength and my salvation.

"Be ye transformed by the renewing of your mind."
—Romans 12:2

Instead of thinking of those old concepts of failure, disease, fear, poverty, and rejection, we are to replace those thoughts with positive thoughts: perfect health, prosperity, abundance, harmony, success, liberty, gratitude, generosity, happiness, and peace.

Renewing the mind is not only spiritual—it is also physical. Some mystics would say it is only a spiritual act. Some believe that when the spiritual mind is renewed, the channel of creative energy automatically renews the body, thus renewing the mind. My spiritual guides have informed me that it is both spiritual and physical. We can renew our minds through prayer and meditation. We can work on the spiritual part daily, but neglecting the physical part opens the door for malnutrition of the physical body. Our physical bodies require a certain amount of nutrition that is wholesome and free of plastic, chemicals, and toxins. In this section, I am referring to the renewing of the mind as mental healing. I must remind you that this is a conscious act.

Mental healing is bound by the same universal laws of mind and spirit, and it is achieved through thoughts. These thoughts are a mental acceptance of the truth. The body is healed as truth transforms our minds. However, we must care for the physical body by providing proper nutrition and protection from harmful toxins.

Remember that conflict of thought will bring about an absence of faith. Faith is that substance that we live by daily in the Word. As our thoughts are opened and we accept the vision of eternity within ourselves—as well as on the other side—we are born again into a new life by the Spirit of God.

"But we all, with open face beholding as in a glass the glory of the Lord, are changed into the same image from glory to glory, even as by the Spirit of the Lord" (II Cor. 3:18).

Our minds are renewed. We are changed by this truth into a newness of life. Christians often call this process "being born again."

The Mind of Jesus

"To be made new in the attitude of your minds; and to put the new self, created to be like God in true righteousness and holiness". (Eph. 4:23–24) Whatever, we think in our minds and firmly believes in forms a new thought pattern within. Whatever thought pattern is held takes outward form in new creations for us.

We are to let the mind be in us which was in Christ Jesus. (Phil. 2:5-6-13) Here we are speaking of the mind of the infinite one. To have the same kind of mind that Jesus spoke of implies a power which is instilled in all and may be accessible by all. This mind is the mind of truth, the divine mind of the Creator, the eternal energy that rules the universe.

Christ said, "A man must be born again if he is to enter the kingdom of God." This meaning is of course is spiritual. We all know that we cannot go back into the womb. This transformation is a new mind, a new attitude, and a new knowledge. An evolutionary process takes place in the mind, which brings about a change in the thought process, creating an awakened or enlightened person. This leaves man standing on the leading edge of thought at all times.

The infinite one will supply all our needs (Phil. 4:8–13). The most wonderful thing about this statement is that it is so true. If we can focus on the truth and devote our lives to the truth, we can be fed from the warehouse of the universe. The warehouse supplies peace, wellness, love, happiness, kindness, and abundance. All is ours for truth shall abide within us.

Constant Prayer and Meditation

"We should pray without ceasing."- 1 Thessalonians 5:17 I believe that this is a constant recognition of our connection to the eternal presence within our soul. To pray without ceasing must surely mean to never doubt and to put all trust and faith in the infinite one. My God is constantly on my mind, yet it is impossible to physically pray without ceasing. It is clear that this is an inner communion with the spirit and the mind.

Meditation brings us closer to this connection at any given moment. I see prayer as speaking to the infinite—intuitively, spiritually, or physically. Meditation, I believe, is a way to listen to God. It opens the mind to spiritual realms. It gives time for reflection and listening rather than asking, talking, and making partitions for life. At times, we all need to stop and listen to our inner spirit for understanding and guidance. In these tranquil moments, we often find peace, love, wellness, prosperity, and all that we are looking for within us.

The first thing that I learned to do in the process of healing my mind and body was to meditate. Many of my relatives and friends looked at me in awe. Even some of my Christian friends and cynical acquaintances looked at me and said, "Really? Yeah, right. Really, Terry?" Others were accepting or curious about meditation.

My sweet ninety-two-year-old grandmother called me a witch. I had gone against all the traditional beliefs that she had been taught as a child—and she would have none of that. There would be no independent thinking in our home. If you do that, the devil must be in you. Bless her soul—I have nothing but love for her. Nonetheless, without sounding redundant, I want to explain in simpler terms exactly what meditation is. To me, meditation is the process of relaxing the mind and body in order to quietly go within the self. For this to happen, one must be in a quiet and safe place—free of distractions.

There are various meditative techniques. However, I have discovered that quiet, concentration, and comfort are the three keys to settling the mind and the body. When this happens, the spirit can begin to listen. At times, interaction takes place with your higher consciousness. Meditation allows the mind to recognize other aspects of its identity.

Suppression of the mind is not the object of meditation; calming the personality allows the mind to freely examine the various aspects of its own consciousness. I would suggest investing in an Eastern or Western meditation technique manual.

If the mind is filled with clutter, there is no room for spirit. We must learn to empty our minds so that spirit may enter. Have you heard that you cannot fill a glass that is already full?

"When people are completely focused on what's wrong and their symptoms, they will perpetuate it. The healing will not occur until they shift their attention from being sick to being well. Because that is the law of attraction."

—**Bob Doyle**

I AM TODAY ALL THAT I WILL EVER BE

I affirm that I am an eternal light.
I affirm that all my energy is positive.
I affirm that the light within is of the infinite one.
I affirm that I am all today that I will ever be.

One thing that I learned though my studies in the seminary is that what a person is today is revealed by the light within them. I am all that I will ever be today—and all that I am ever going to be. The truth I carry within me—whether it is light or darkness—is already within me. I am the true light that brings forth reality.

I have the power within me to heal myself as well as others. I have the power within me to manifest my desires. I am a co-creator of my destiny and all my life experiences. Though I am an educator of metaphysics, I also have experienced psychic phenomena. Some of it has been impressive—and some has not—but all have been phenomenal. We expect metaphysicality to be so solemn. We speak with reverence when we meet someone with the capacity to bridge dimensions. They are no different than you or me. They possess a gift of extreme freedom—a freedom that most have not yet learned to utilize—and a gift of oneness with true energy.

An Embodiment of Memory

When I meditate, a universal light warms my inner being—and I connect with the oneness of time. I once read that Einstein said that linear time is an invention of man. It was developed to help man feel focused in his space.

The inner light and time has everything to do with each other. In the beginning, there was no time—only space. In the beginning, there was energy, which is the light. The light has always been the light. Our spiritual memory of home is already instilled in us. We are each an embodiment of our memory—whether we understand it or not. Time does not exist at home or here. It is something that we made up for our shallow understanding. Having said this, it should be understood that home is perfection. There is no sickness, sadness, war, poverty, or anything like the time and space we have created on earth.

If Einstein was correct in thinking that all time is occurring simultaneously, then so is our total experience in life. If all this is true, and I believe that it is, we can choose to create our own reality. We are selecting from many possible energy points—some are harmonic and others are not—that put us in touch with the reasons we are here in the first place. These reasons are, in fact, learning experiences that teach us what we need to resolve in our reality.

Our true self is mere energy, which is pure light. When we arrive home, there will be no need for the sun or lamps for light. "There will be no more night. They will not need the light of a lamp or the light of the sun, for the Lord God will give them light" (Rev. 22:5).

As heirs of the other side, we are like Him, pure energy, light, and eternal in spirit. If we are to be like Him, we must become more like Him if we wish to draw a greater good into our lives. There is no limit to the mind of the infinite one—it fills all space in the universe. Nonetheless, there does appear to be a limit to man's understanding of the infinite one, time, and space.

As our understanding unfolds, our possibilities of manifestation increase. We attract unto ourselves from our thoughts. The universal law in which we operate is truly infinite; however, man appears to be finite due to the fact he has not yet evolved enough to truly understand his own self.

Understanding Power

If we are pure energy and light like him, we are also perfect in spirit like him. When we attempt to heal our bodies, it is not the physical body that we are attempting to heal—we are attempting to heal the thoughts that bind us into a prison of limitation, which is not of the infinite one.

Ernest Holmes said, "The spiritual man needs no healing, health is omnipresent reality, and when the obstruction that hinder healing is removed, it will be found that health was there all the time." This power is not our own. It is the power of the infinite one within.

"I heard a voice from the throne saying, 'Now the dwelling of God is with men, and He will live with them. There will be no more death or mourning or crying or pain, for the old order of things has passed away'" (Rev. 21:3–4). This is one of those mystical sayings of Jesus that must be carefully considered before accepting it. What exactly is Jesus talking about here? I believe that Jesus is referring to the willingness to lose a personal sense of responsibility when we let go of the thought of isolation and claim a real unity with the infinite one. At that time, we lose the personal and find the universal. I have learned through spirit that we are only as powerful as we unite with the power of the Infinite Source of life.

A false belief indicates that one must give up all pleasure and benefits in life. These ideas are as far from the truth as possible. The false belief that we must be unhappy, starving, or indigent in order to serve and worship him is totally false. These immature ideas deny our divine birthright of the incarnate spirit.

If You Can Lose Self, Nothing Shall Be Impossible

And when they were come to the multitude, there came to him a certain man, kneeling down to him, saying, Lord have mercy on my son: for he is a lunatic, and sore vexed: for often he falleth into the fire, and into the water. And I brought him to thy disciples, and they could not cure him. Then Jesus answered and said, O faithless and perverse generation, how long shall I be with you! How long shall I suffer you! Bring him hither to me. And Jesus rebuked the devil; and he departed out of him: and the child was

> *cured from that very hour. Then came the disciple to Jesus apart, and said, Why could not we cast him out? And Jesus said unto them, Because of your belief: for verily I say unto you, if ye have faith as a grain of mustard seed, ye shall say unto mountains, remove hence to yonder place, and it shall remove, and nothing shall be impossible unto you. How be it this kind go not out but by prayer and fasting. (Matthew 17)*

Holy Scripture states that we can do the same things that Jesus did. We can perform miracles in his name. If one can lose the smallest indicator of self and find the greater spiritual man—the incarnated and real truth—one can find a path to true awakening of the eternal light, blessed healing energy. This light illumines the road of the personal when there are no obstructions. If you can only lose self, you can gain the whole world without limitations says the spirit of the infinite. The infinite one plays no favorites. The law of the universe cannot change its own nature. We know that the light in which we grow in spirit brings about an evolutionary breakthrough in our thoughts. Fasting and prayer can bring thoughts closer to reality—not because of the mere act of fasting and praying, but because it opens up the windows of receptivity in our minds.

Remember that time has no place in reference to the infinite. Whatever we are in the future, we are today. It is just a matter of evolving into our own. Sometimes we ask God for something material and wait for it without realizing that we already have what we asked for. Sometimes we just have to learn how to access our blessings.

We have been given the power to manifest our needs through thoughts. We just haven't realized it yet; therefore, we wait until we evolve enough to access what we want. If we can only awaken to know and understand that if we desire positive energy in any way, we already have it. God is with us always.

"I've seen kidneys regenerate. I've seen cancer dissolved. I've seen eyesight improve and come back."

—**Michael Bernard Beckwith**

OTHERS SEE PROBLEMS, I SEE OPPORTUNITY AND GROWTH

> I affirm that what I have experienced has made me.
> I affirm that all I am is due to my experiences.
> I affirm that I created my experiences.
> I affirm that every problem is an opportunity in life.

Many years ago, I would have freaked over losing a job, someone stealing items out of my home, having a car repossessed, losing a child to illness or an accident, or a losing a parent or loved one. Over the years, my mind has evolved into understanding the consciousness of the permanency of the omnipresent substance as it abides in me. I realize that this is a strong statement to make in such matters of material goods and of the heart.

I want to encourage a positive attitude towards a transcendent visualization of yourself and your life that faith has brought into your being, enduring and steadfast; so that when our economy collapse, the banks take the money and run, your home is in foreclosure, you are ill with no health insurance, your spouse runs off with the babysitter, your loved ones die, there is no money for food, even your dog dies, there is still in our finances and mind a consciousness of the permanency of the omnipresent substance that abide in us. We still maintain the power to co-create our reality through thought. "You" are in charge of your life, not your circumstances.

In *Prosperity*, Charles Fillmore said, "If we have freely received, we must freely give and keep substance going, confident in our understanding that our supply is unlimited and that it is always right at hand in the omnipresent Mind of God. In this understanding we can stand the loss of outrageous fortunes, depression and financial failures and still see God as abundant substance waiting to come into manifestation."

> *Put on the whole armor of God that ye may be able to withstand in the evil days ... for we fight not against flesh and blood but against principalities, against powers, against rulers of the darkness of the world, against spiritual wickedness in high places. Wherefore take unto you the whole armor of God that ye may be able to stand in the evil day, and having done all to stand. Stand therefore, having your loins girt with truth, and having on the breastplate of righteousness; And your feet shod with the preparation of the gospel of peace; Above all, taking the shield of faith, wherewith ye shall be able to quench all the fiery darts of the wicked. And take the helmet of salvation and the sword of the spirit, which is the Word of God. (Ephesians 6)*

When Trouble Arrives, Put on a New Mind

All my life, I have been told to renew my mind through prayer. I'm going to take this a little further and recommend renewing your mind during times of hardship through the spirit and putting on the new man, which is created in pure spirit and holiness. The mind is the creative spring that is at work within us.

The mind takes its blueprint from spirit and automatically renews the physical man in purity and holiness. Therefore, where others see problems, I see growth and opportunity. Whatever the mind holds and firmly thinks or believes forms a new pattern of thought within its creative element. The thoughts that are held in the mind take on a form of itself. It becomes an outward form in a new creation. This process is often called manifestation. Many have written books on this manifestation, but all enlightened people have been blessed with this knowledge and ability by the infinite one. If you have been awakened, you are well aware of the gift of manifestation.

In a sermon on May 1, 2011, Pastor Henry Babers said, "I do not know how everything is going to come together, but I stand from within with confidence that everything is going to work out."

His theme—standing with confidence—renewed my confidence in him as a pastor, which teaches the truth as the Holy Spirit reveals it to him. I know that he understands spirit more that he reveals on Sunday mornings. That sermon reminded the congregation that we are what we think and what we believe. Knowing that I am all today that I will ever be renewed my faith.

The good things that have happened to me have made me who I am today. The negative things that have happened to me have made me who I am today. When problems arise, I know that I have allowed this negativity into my life for a reason. I stand for the infinite one in my belief that everything is taken care of and will work out just as it should. I am strengthened in confidence and in faith. I rejoice for the opportunity to stand. I have often told my higher power that if He sends me, I will go. I would do whatever job He had for me. This is a process of standing. Standing brings growth, prosperity, perfect health, happiness, enlightenment, and confidence in the infinite.

When problems arrive in our lives, we must create new outcomes in our minds of how we want things to turn out. We have the power to create our futures and thank the infinite source for our past.

Everything that you are is made because of who you were at any moment in time. Every experience you have ever had has made you who you are today. Every stressful moment, hard time, grief, or pain has brought you to this moment as the person you are today. You have taken all those hard times and sad moments and turned them into who you are today.

Only a weak person cannot evolve over the years through life experiences. If you cannot learn and grow from your own experiences, what can you learn from? How can you grow? Every problem in life is an opportunity for growth, healing, prosperity, peace, wholeness, and manifestation.

"Anything we focus on, we do create. So if we're really angry, for instance, at a war that's going on, or strife, or suffering, we're adding our energy to it. We're pushing ourselves, and that only creates resistance."

—**Hale Dwoskin**

HOW DO I KNOW WHEN MY HIGHER CONSCIOUSNESS IS TALKING TO ME?

> I affirm that spirit speaks to me.
> I affirm that he is not only real in
> my life but all around me.
> I affirm that the Word is in my own mouth.
> I affirm that I am made from life and I am life.

There has never been a more humbling moment in my life than when I recognized the pure, holy, profound information that was being given to me by spirit. It was a moment of awakening that can never be forgotten. It had happened many times in the past, but I was unaware of the truth of the presence.

I have experienced spirits communicating intuitively, speaking out loud just like person-to-person communication, a smell of familiarity, a gentle touch, or an overwhelming hair-standing-up feeling. I have been blessed with the gift of sight; I can actually see forms of spirit. When my higher consciousness speaks or communicates in any way, I know his voice. There is no doubt in my mind who is talking or communicating to me. The Bible states that the sheep knows its master's voice.

Christopher asked, "Mom, how do I know when he is talking to me? What do I need to do to hear him?"

His questions were so innocent, authentic, and genuine. The answers that he was seeking were right there inside of him. He had not taken the time to listen. Sometimes we get so caught up and busy with our daily lives that we have not found time to listen to our higher power. He speaks to us daily. Life is from within out—never from without in. Sometimes we need to quiet our thoughts, minds, businesses, and take time out for him. I call this time meditation and prayer. The more we take time to listen to him, the more we can hear, see, feel, and even smell his presence. He is a constant guide in our lives—nothing is by chance. We are made in his image, and we are forever connected to him. The Word is in our own mouth. The Word is truly our own being.

Ernest Holmes said, "The Word is our belief in life and when that word is one with life it is life." If we take the time to feel the connection to the infinite one, it will change our lives forever.

Spirit Knows Spirit

According to the Holy Spirit, spirit knows spirit. There is no need to place a face on it. Faces are for man's comfort and understanding—not for spirit. The infinite creative spirit has imparted his life to man. We are made from life—and we are life. We are pure spirit, living as avatars on earth.

Jesus Christ said, "I am the Way, the truth and the Life."

When I read this scripture it reminded me of a parallel teaching of Jesus and Moses. Moses told us that the Word was in our own mouth—and Jesus taught that the kingdom of heaven is within man. Therefore, all we need to do is listen. "Man know thyself ... the eternal God is thy refuge, and underneath are the everlasting arms."- Deuteronomy 33:27

No attempt has been made to explain everything that the Bible says. Many statements are taken literally, but its teaching is of a world of spiritual realization far beyond what the everyday person can began to conceive. The full meaning of the revelations of the Holy Spirit can never be absolutely clear or fully understood until we have experienced an awakening to the truth. Even then, there are years of studying, educating, and meditating on the truth.

The Infinite One Speaks to the Heart

Words are powerful when the mind listens to the heart. For some unknown reason, our hearts can reach a depth that the intellect can never penetrate. It must be understood that no matter how intellectually or analytically correct a person may be, they must have a deep feeling and sincere conviction that can penetrate the soul enabling one to communicate with the invisible. This invisible is the truth—the spirit—of I Am.

Through self-realization, we learn to listen to the stillness of our minds, which listen to the heart. The true creative power of the mind is far deeper in substance and true form than any shallow ideas of the intellectual. Without this sincere conviction within one's heart and mind, all that a person can experience is what they see—which is without depth or truth or any real substance. The feelings, emotions and thoughts are the true creative force in our universe.

If we can understand how the mind speaks to our hearts, we can understand the true force that communes with the spirit. We are in constant company with the infinite one. If the universal law is our mind in action—and we realize this law through our feelings, emotions, and thoughts—we must consciously know that we are guided continually into the right actions for our lives. Within our minds and hearts, we must know that intelligence exists and is always with us to make our way plain and joyous. When he speaks, we feel him. We may deny this feeling or intuitive guidance, but he speaks and guides us. After all, we do have free will. He will never impose his will upon us—we have to accept it freely.

Jesus taught that we are spiritual beings in a spiritual universe. Jesus discovered the secret to life, love, and ultimate power. During his time on earth, he proved his power beyond any doubt. He is known from one end of the earth to the other. He raised the dead, taught of everlasting life, and commanded the elements. He profoundly proved his power; it only makes sense that we follow his example and teaching.

Every man wants to believe that something in this universe will make him live forever—and be happy, prosperous, healthy, and whole mentally. Man looks for something that will cause him to be safe and secure. Divine energy created all and provided the happiness and completeness that man is constantly searching for. Supreme energy governs the universe and everything therein; it is not far away. Its presence is something that is right now—here with us—at this very moment.

Can We Actually Talk to God?

We know, most of us talk at our God or Supreme Being. Having an actual conversation with the infinite is a different proposition. When we look at the word "communicate," we are talking about information being sent out, received by the receiver, processed, and reciprocated. In physical time, there can be no real communication without reciprocity of thought. So unless you have a two-way communication process taking place between you and the infinite, you certainly cannot talk to God.

The infinite communicate with us through dreams, visions, intuitive feelings, signs, and through talking. He is alive and working within all living creatures. There is an actual vibratory frequency that some of us are capable of connecting to. This connection allows one to connect with the other side when they choose to communicate. We call these people mediums, priests, prophets, metaphysicians, ministers, evangelists, preachers, gurus, or the Dalai Lama. God is a universal principle, intelligence, and ultimate power. We think of this force as an essence and energy within all.

It is often difficult for the finite to understand the infinite in terms of universal law. We do not want to lose the personal sense of contact with this invisible power. We should always remember that the connection with the infinite is part of ourselves. At times, we feel our consciousness merge with the universal as one. At other times, we may feel that we are left alone or that our God has abandoned us. When we communicate, we communicate with the infinite source. Our bodies are the temple of the infinite source.

"We're all connected. We just don't see it. There isn't an 'out there' and an 'in here.' Everything in the universe is connected. It is just one energy field."

—**John Assaraf**

THE QUEST: AN AWAKENING

I affirm that I am awakened to the truth.
I affirm that the truth dwells within me.
I affirm that I live within a positive light.
I affirm that I am on the path of enlightenment.

The spirit responds to us by connecting to our state of thought. It can only connect through our thoughts to the degree in which we comprehend it. We are in a constant state of evolution, forever evolving into a higher state of consciousness. Prayer, communion with the Holy Spirit, meditation and contemplation are processes we use to connect our minds with the ultimate source energy. This process opens the channels for thought to take place; this creates or manifests our reality.

The more we receive and comprehend the spirit, the more it moves through us. It does not matter whether we are dealing with physics or metaphysics—we are forever on an infinite quest that involves the laws of the universe. We are dealing with a very powerful force or spirit. It is evident that spirit is capricious and is forever creating and changing the laws of nature and the universe; after all, the law is a servant unto spirit.

Demonstration of the Quest

When we look at the practical application of the laws set before us in the universe, we are really demonstrating pure thought. This practical application is a growth process in our evolutionary state. We are each a part of this infinite life energy that is forever growing, expanding, and reaching new dimensions.

The Holy Spirit is infinite, incarnating itself within all living creatures. We shall never stop growing, progressing or expanding. There are no limitations to our creativeness. There shall never be a time that our minds stop progressing—even when we reach the other side. I believe that often when we get home, we are reincarnated again and again in hopes of getting it right. We are forever on this quest of truth. When we finally reach our goal of true awakening, the Hindus say that we would have reach the supreme they call Brahman.

Our quest should always be that of the truth. When people reach a certain age, they often set out on a quest for the truth as it is known or understood to them. Others have no concept of such things and do not desire to know any more than they knew as infants.

Sometimes our eyes open at the strangest times. Pastor Elder Lau'chie from my Michigan home ministry said, "The eyes are the windows of the world. What a person opens up to self will be a part of them always."

I believe that the spirit of the most high infinite consciousness is in wind, waves, lava, and mountains. Spirit manifests its presence through all of nature. It manifests through the minds and hearts of man. It proclaims light in the darkness and life where there is destitution.

During your quest, you will find that you are surrounded by the ultimate intelligence, which is law. This intelligence receives the impressions of our thoughts and acts upon them as we think. This knowledge and action should be as natural for mankind as it is to fall on your knees in thanksgiving and gratitude. This natural universal law is a part of man, whether or not he accepts it and believes it.

Religion

During my quest, I began to believe that the infinite one has touched every culture in respect to religion. We have different customs in religious practices—but the same goal. I believe in every religion that teaches love, light, peace, forgiveness, strength, sound mind, and eternity with the infinite. I believe this because it is an avenue for people to worship God. I believe in my own religion more than I believe in any other because this is the practice through which I worship the infinite one. Nonetheless, we must listen with our hearts and minds—and not so much our ears—to hear the truth. Man will always put self in the information that is being provided.

How can I attempt to take another man's deity? Should I attempt to replace it with my own? The infinite speaks to us all. He speaks to our hearts and our minds. Sometimes he speaks to our souls. How can I interpret what he said to my brother or sister? I can only tell you what he said to me. When analyzing the messages, it becomes clear that there are many correlations and themes. The message is always the same—despite our cultural differences and misinterpretations.

Religion, the discovery of the truth, is an awakening of the mind to become free to listen to the inner voice within. Making a commitment to search for enlightenment does not mean that one has to give up life. It only means that one must sacrifice self by letting go of the "me syndrome." We must join that inner energy.

In the midst of a large crowd, a diseased woman touched Jesus. Jesus was aware of the woman's presence and said, "Thou faith has made thee whole." –Luke 8:46

I believe that this was a lesson in impersonal healing. It is clear that spiritual-minded persons possess a wholeness and completeness in all things. Spirituality brings the gift of manifestation, prosperity, healing, wisdom, happiness, gratitude, generosity, peace, and selflessness.

Thought

The gift of manifestation is a universal law—set in motion through thought. This law is in line with holy teachings that "it is done unto men as they believe." Holy Scripture says, "As a man thinketh, so is he." – Proverbs 23:7

If we can think positively and in good report, we can accomplish all things. We can do this because the Holy Spirit dwells in our inner minds. We know this spirit as the creator of heaven and earth and all that dwells within. We have been taught from infancy that God will supply all our needs. Whether we accept it or not, believe it or not, if you think it, you will create it. The universal law knows only to provide what we ask for or think of.

"And you can break yourself free from your hereditary patterns, cultural codes, social beliefs, and prove once and for all that the power within you is greater than the power within the world."

—**Michael Bernard Beckwith**

SMUDGING AND CLEANSING RITUALS

I affirm that positive energy is always around me.
I affirm that my life is clean and free from clutter.
Whether it is spiritual or physical, I am pure.

People ask, "What is smudging? Isn't that an Indian ritual? Is it messy?"

Smudging is about purifying energy that exists around people, places, and things. This is done by performing a smoke ritual. Smudging has been used by many cultures during ceremonial purification and protection rituals. Cherokees, Lakotas, Catholics, Eastern Orthodox churches, pre-Christian pagans, Hindus, and Buddhists use smudging.

When I smudge, I begin by wafting the smoke in all areas to be cleansed, paying close attention to dark corners and closets. I usually chant the kadoish; however, any chant in which one would have faith would do. Cedar, tobacco, sweet grass, red willow, calamus, dogwood, and white sage can be used for smudging. White sage is the most commonly used herb for purification.

It is believed that the smoke attaches itself to the negative energy; as the smoke dissipates, it takes negative energy from its present state to regenerate into positive energy. Practitioners believe that burning white sage actually changes the ionization polarity within the air. Since smoke rises, always start at the lowest level of the building or home when smudging. It is advisable to open a window or door during the smudging ritual. This helps with the visualization of negative energy leaving the area to be purified.

Another tool I use is sea salt. I use sea salt for the outside of my home. I pour the sea salt along the edge of my home as I walk entirely around it. It is important to pay extra attention to windows, doors, and ventilation ducts. As I sprinkle the salt, I ask the ultimate source or the Holy Spirit to protect my home from all negative energy and activity. I usually use a specific prepared affirmation for this ritual. I say, "Twenty feet out, twenty feet around, twenty feet up, twenty feet down—no negative energy within these grounds."

I encircle myself in the white light of the Holy Spirit with divine protection, love, and tranquility.

Water

Another negative energy purifier is water. I take a glass of spring or purified water and make essence water. I leave the essence water in the room to be cleansed overnight. During a twenty-four-hour period, numerous bubbles appear in the water. After the cleansing period, flush the water down the drain or toilet. The bubbles are negative energy being pulled together in the essence water.

Bells

Bells have been used for centuries by Christians, Buddhists, and Hindus as a cleansing tool. The ringing of bells is good for cleansing crystals—as well as clearing negative energy from a building or home.

Father Errol Harvey lit white candles during the blessing of our home. As he lit the candles, he chanted an affirmation and rang high-pitched bells throughout the house. My husband and I asked why he used bells, and he told us he used them to scare off evil spirits.

I use bells to clean my crystals. I find bells work just as well as sunlight, moonlight, salt, and warm soapy water. After a cleaning, I hear the crystals' humming vibrations while I hold them. It is an awesome feeling.

"The teaching of Jesus was based on the theory that we are surrounded by an intelligent law, which does unto each as he believes. Jesus said, 'As ye believe, it shall be done unto you.'"

—Ernest Holmes (1887–1960)

A TRANSCENDENT EXPERIENCE WITH THE INFINITE

> I affirm that my body is filled with
> a euphoric electrical light.
> I affirm that during meditation and prayer.
> I can hear, feel, and see the infinite one clearly.

In order for me to describe a transcendent type of experience, I'm going to introduce you to Kundalini. It is understood that the energy is merely the inward energy of the soul. Energy leaves the body when the flesh ceases to live. It is a universal consciousness present in all living beings. It is that creative power that dwells within. It is said to be that self-realization, enlightenment, God-consciousness, nirvana, and Kundalini awakening are all the same energy from within. All of this power is usually discovered during meditation. It is considered the opening of the third eye, bringing one closer to the infinite.

All religions in this world and the next have—and always will have—a group of devoted followers that seek a direct, transcendent experience with the ultimate source.

They excuse themselves from the fundamentalist scriptural or dogmatic teachings in order to experience the divine. This is done through meditation. There is one unique thing about this experience: they all end up describing the exact same thing after the experience is over.

An energy source fills the entire being with a euphoric energy of electricity starting from the base of the spine. The Buddhists call this energy chi, the Japanese call it the Ki, the Balinese call it taksu, Christians call it the Holy Spirit, the Kalahari bushmen call it the "Kia", and the Islamic Sufis call it the "The Beloved."

The most import thing to remember is to let go of self. Without releasing the self or the intellect, one cannot experience the overwhelming electrical euphoric energy.

Spirit Will Love You through It All

Through constant, devoted meditation and prayer, I have learned to tap into the energy of the infinite. Sometimes the pictures are clear to me—as are the voices and intuitive guidance. At other times, I can't really tune in to the correct vibration of spirit. That is when I find myself giving in to the flesh. I find myself in a constant state of rebirth and growth. I am forever evolving into a higher spiritual being. Spirit came to me during meditation and said, "I will love you through it all." As my soul overflowed with an overwhelming feeling of love and joy, I felt safe from all worldly negativity, anger, hurt, and harm. I felt safe knowing that nothing in this world can harm me if it is not meant to be from the foundation of time.

I have the power of the infinite within me—to heal, prophesy, create, manifest, forgive, love, and move mountains. "I say to you, if you have faith the size of a mustard seed, you will say to this mountain, 'Move from here to there,' and it will move. Nothing will be impossible for you" (Mathew 17:20).

The Coming of the Spirit

> *When the time for Pentecost was fulfilled, they were all in one place together. And suddenly there came from the sky a noise like a strong driving wind, and it filled the entire house in which they were. Then there appeared to them tongues as of fire, which parted and came to rest on each one of them. And they were all filled with the Holy Spirit and began to speak in different tongues, as the spirit enabled them to proclaim." (Acts 2:1–4)*

Christians believe in the descending of the Holy Spirit upon a person. The spirit channels information through the person or informs them of events or future information.

Control through Thoughts

I have been shown that I have the control of conditions within my life through the power of mind. My body is the temple of the infinite, and he truly dwells within me. Holy Scriptures affirm that when man is in harmony with the infinite, he automatically prospers. The word of life is an emancipation of the soul from the thralldom of negativity—otherwise known as evil—and every lack or limitation thereof.

My spirit tells me that from the teachings of Moses, through the divine inspiration of the Major Prophets, culminating in the luminous mind of the Christ, given the thought of I Am, the truth is reiterated. If we live in faith and truth of spirit, everything we touch or think of will prosper.

I am living proof of the Word. Like so many others, I was raised without a mother or father. My grandmother raised my sister and me as a single parent in so many ways. Living in Detroit in the midst of heavy gang activity, life was not easy. It took constant conversations with my higher consciousness, pleading for guidance, help, and love in an environment of chaos and negative energy. I lived so much of my life in search of the truth and the transcendent experience with my God. I prayed that God would hold my hand and guide me through my life as a child. I prayed that I may know him fully through divine wisdom from the Holy Spirit. I prayed for proof of the living God so I could abandon my fear-based worship and evolve into a higher consciousness with the living "I Am."

He is within me and I am within him. He lives within my heart and my soul. I am healed from the inside out. I am as creative as he said I would be. I am happy and carefree. His words live within me. I have experienced this transcendent universal energy. I hear his voice at different times. I feel his intuitive guidance more often than others do. I see his presence during meditation and often at unexpected times. I can often smell his closeness in the stillness of the day. It is often so sweet that flowers have nothing to offer in its place. The illuminated presence of the Holy Spirit can lead anyone to believe that they are out of their minds.

This clairvoyant experience usually awakens the higher consciousness within our minds, leaving an impact of true spiritual enlightenment.

When I speak of this transcendent experience with the infinite, I am speaking of matters that deal with the spiritual realms of this world. I am talking about a very different world that that we can see with our physical eyes. Nonetheless, it is more real than our physical world. I'm not talking about emotions. I'm speaking about the actual experience of sound, vision, smell, and touch. I'm not referencing to talking at the infinite—I'm referring to having a dialogue either through intuitive guidance, clairaudience, clairvoyance, clairsentience, or inspirational thoughts.

"I am nothing alone. I do nothing. The Holy Spirit works through me and accomplishes all through me."

—**Aaron Harvey**

AWAKEN!

AWAKEN!

AWAKEN!

Prayers and Affirmations for Self-Help

Within these short affirmations, I have tried to set a stage for healing—whether it is mental, physical, or spiritual.

I am not proclaiming any occult power in these words. The only power is already within you since the infinite source of life dwells within you. He has all the power—you only have to ask for it through true meditation and prayer. One must put the request into his or her vibration.

He Is Mighty Within Me to Heal
Ernest Holmes 1887-1960

God within me is mighty to heal.
He healeth me of all my diseases and
removes all fear from me.
My God within is now healing me
of all sickness and pain and
Is bringing comfort to my soul.
God is my life; I cannot be sick.
I hear the voice of truth telling me to
arise and walk, for I am healed.
I am healed.

Come, and Let Me Heal You
Ernest Holmes 1887-1960

Come and I will heal you.
The inner power of life within me is God,
And God has all power.
I will heal and help all who come to me.
I know that the realization of life and love within me
Heal all who come into its presence.
I silently bless all who enter my atmosphere.
It is not I, but the Father who dwelleth in me,
He doeth the work.
I heal all who come near me.

I Acknowledge the True God Within
Dr. Terry A. Harvey, PhD, DD

I am so grateful for your presence in my life.
I affirm that I am wise and knowledgeable.
I acknowledge that you speak through me.
I affirm that I am healthy and perfectly well
In every way.
I acknowledge the true God within

My Life Is for Your Service
Dr. Terry A. Harvey, PhD, DD

I affirm that my life is for your service
and the good of mankind.
I affirm, through your presence, I have learned
to manifest my reality through thought.
I affirm that I know no limits to my wisdom nor
bounty that has been bestowed upon me.
I affirm that I may do more for others
than I may do for myself.
I affirm that my life is for your service

I Am A Co-Creator Of My Reality
Dr. Terry A. Harvey PhD, DD

I affirm that the infinite energy
within me has all power to
Co-create my reality.
I can do nothing alone, without the
power of the one who sent me,
I am powerless.
I am cocreator of all that I desire and believe that is mine.
I am prosperous, healthy, wise, and happy.
Strong in mind and in spirit
I am generous, forgiving, and most of all
compassionate and filled with infinite love.
I am co-creator of my reality

I Affirm that Jesus Is the Greatest Mystic of All Time
Dr. Terry A. Harvey, PhD, DD

I affirm that Jesus is one of the greatest mystics that
Has ever walked the face of the earth.
I will choose to follow his path and teachings.
I affirm that the great I Am is still speaking to us today.
He is still creating spirits like Jesus
that can heal, see the future,
And, yes, walk on water.
I shall forever have an open mind
And discern the sprit that lives within me.
I affirm that Jesus is the greatest mystic of all time.

I Am All That I Will Ever Be
Dr. Terry A. Harvey, PhD, DD

I am all that I will ever be.
The infinite source of life knows no time.
On the other side, time does not exist.
There are no fortuitous moments in life.

I Worship God Everywhere

I bow to the one Infinite Father, differently manifesting in the many churches and temples that have all been erected in His honor. I worship the one God resting on the various altars of different teachings and religious faiths.

Paramhansa Yoganada

I Am Not Alone

I am not alone, for a Presence goes with me and daily accompanies me on my travels. Always I shall find this Divine Companion with me. He will not desert me nor allow me to go alone. He will always be with me and near me, and will always provide for my every want. My life is His with Christ in God.

Ernest Holmes 1887-1960

My Beloved is Calling Me

By realizing God I shall be reclaimed as His child. Without asking begging I shall receive all prosperity, health, and wisdom.

Paramahansa Yoganada

His Eye Is On The Sparrow

"His eye is on the sparrow and I know he watches me". This is a blessed thought, for it means that we cannot wander from his Presence, nor depart from His care. Always He will watch over us and comfort us. Forever we shall sit in His house and ceaselessly He will care for us. The All-Seeing Eye cannot overlook anyone, and all shall be kept in His care.

Ernest Holmes 1887-1960

Overcoming Fear and Worry

God is within me, around me, protecting me, so I will banish the gloom of fear that shuts out His guiding light and makes me stumble into ditches of error.

I will wipe away, with the soothing veil of Divine Mother's peace, the dream fears of disease, sadness, and ignorance. Teach me to be tenaciously and cautiously courageous instead of often being afraid.

I will fear nothing except myself, when
I try to deceive my conscience.

Paramahansa Yoganada

INDEX

A

affirmations 6, 32, 45, 119
Angels 20, 37
Atman 11
Avatars 30, 52, 96
Awakenings 6

B

bible ix, xv, 2, 7, 8, 12, 14, 29, 33, 42, 44, 45, 47, 53, 55, 59, 96, 97
Brahman 10, 11, 48, 102
Buddhism 11

C

chakra system 68, 69
Charles Fillmore 41, 66, 90
Christians 7, 8, 10, 19, 20, 27, 33, 76, 109, 112, 113
co-creators 12, 26, 43
consciously xii, 46, 98
Create xi, xiv, xv, 3, 6, 12, 14, 28, 31, 32, 41, 42, 48, 59, 74, 82, 90, 92, 94, 101, 104, 113, 124
crystal 67, 69, 70, 109

D

death xi, xiii, 7, 20, 22, 32, 48, 55, 59, 64, 84
depression x, 35, 90
Divine Beings xi
dogma ix, 1, 6, 22

E

electromagnetic 11
Empowering xi
enemy 18, 25
Energy x, xi, xii, 1, 2, 3, 4, 6, 8, 10, 12, 13, 17, 27, 28, 29, 32, 35, 36, 46, 51, 52, 53, 54, 59, 60, 67, 68, 70, 71, 75, 77, 81, 82, 83, 85, 94, 98, 99, 100, 101, 102, 104, 107, 108, 109, 111, 112, 114, 124
enlightenment 2, 6, 9, 10, 11, 30, 33, 42, 92, 101, 104, 111, 115
Ernest Holmes 51, 83, 96, 110, 120, 121, 128, 130
evolving xiii, 42, 67, 85, 101, 112

F

faith ix, x, 16, 24, 27, 31, 34, 36, 37, 42, 48, 55, 66, 76, 78, 85, 89, 90, 92, 104, 107, 113, 114

G

gifted xii, 19
God xi, xii, xiii, 1, 2, 3, 6, 7, 8, 9, 10, 11, 12, 14, 18, 20, 21, 22, 24, 25, 26, 28, 29, 31, 34, 36, 37, 38, 42, 44, 45, 51, 54, 59, 60, 69, 76, 77, 78, 83, 84, 85, 90, 97, 99, 103, 104, 111, 114, 120, 121, 122, 127, 128, 129, 131
God-Mind 2
God-Within 26

H

healer x, 2, 33, 38, 52, 53, 67, 69
healing ix, x, xii, 6, 13, 26, 31, 33, 34, 36, 37, 38, 41, 42, 52, 53, 54, 56, 67, 69, 70, 71, 76, 78, 80, 83, 85, 92, 104, 119, 120
heaven 19, 30, 31, 32, 47, 60, 97, 104
Higher Consciousness 1, 2, 13, 24, 45, 46, 62, 79, 95, 114, 115
humanity 10

I

I Am 2, 4, 5, 11, 12, 14, 17, 20, 21, 22, 31, 38, 41, 43, 45, 51, 53, 59, 60, 61, 70, 75, 76, 81, 89, 92, 95, 97, 101, 107, 112, 114, 115, 116, 119, 120, 122, 124, 125, 126, 128
Infinite xi, xii, xiv, xv, 1, 10, 13, 14, 17, 21, 27, 28, 29, 30, 31, 33, 34, 37, 38, 41, 42, 44, 45, 47, 52, 54, 59, 60, 68, 70, 77, 78, 81, 83, 84, 85, 91, 92, 96, 97, 99, 101, 102, 103, 111, 112, 113, 115, 119, 124, 126, 127
Intuition 5
Islamic Sufis 112

J

Japanese 112
Jesus 2, 4, 7, 22, 44, 55, 60, 61, 76, 77, 84, 85, 97, 98, 104, 110, 125
Joan of Arc 20

K

Kalahari Bushmen 112
knowledge xi, 3, 4, 5, 6, 10, 11, 20, 24, 31, 45, 54, 77, 91, 103

L

life ix, x, xi, xii, xv, 2, 3, 4, 10, 11, 13, 14, 19, 21, 22, 24, 25, 26, 27, 29, 30, 31, 32, 34, 36, 41, 42, 43, 44, 46, 47, 48, 52, 53, 54, 55, 59, 60, 62, 64, 67, 71, 76, 78, 81, 82, 84, 89, 90, 91, 92, 95, 96, 98, 102, 103, 104, 107, 113, 119, 120, 121, 122, 123, 126, 128

lost scriptures 7

M

manifestation xii, xv, 14, 27, 28, 32, 34, 41, 43, 83, 90, 91, 92, 104

mankind xi, 6, 18, 29, 31, 54, 103, 123

Mary Magdalene 8

meditation xii, xv, 2, 5, 17, 18, 19, 20, 22, 26, 52, 64, 69, 71, 75, 77, 78, 79, 96, 101, 111, 112, 114, 119

mediums x, 7, 12, 19, 20, 36, 42, 64, 99

mega-ministers 21

metaphysician 5, 42, 54, 56, 71, 99

metaphysics x, 3, 81, 101

Michael Bernard Beckwith xii, 19, 38, 46, 47, 50, 88, 106

mind xii, xiii, 1, 2, 3, 4, 5, 8, 9, 10, 13, 17, 18, 21, 25, 26, 29, 30, 31, 33, 35, 36, 38, 41, 42, 43, 44, 46, 48, 51, 52, 55, 58, 60, 64, 69, 72, 75, 76, 78, 79, 83, 85, 89, 90, 91, 92, 96, 97, 98, 101, 102, 103, 104, 113, 114, 115, 124, 125

Moses 11, 97, 114

Muslim 10, 11, 27, 48

mysticism x, 3, 25

N

New Age 12

New Thought 11, 36, 60, 76

Nirvana 11, 111

O

Other Side 32, 48, 62, 70, 76, 83, 99, 102, 126

P

persecutions 6, 8

positive xiv, xv, 26, 27, 30, 32, 37, 42, 44, 55, 75, 81, 86, 89, 101, 107, 108

prosperity xii, xiv, 6, 13, 21, 22, 26, 36, 41, 43, 52, 64, 75, 78, 90, 92, 104, 129

prosperous xii, 2, 41, 51, 59, 98, 124

psychic x, 12, 20, 36, 42, 47, 64, 81

R

reality 1, 3, 5, 6, 11, 12, 14, 18, 26, 28, 30, 31, 32, 41, 42,

43, 45, 46, 47, 53, 81, 82, 83, 85, 90, 101, 123, 124
reincarnation 7, 32, 33, 55
religious ix, xi, xii, 1, 2, 6, 10, 20, 25, 46, 51, 52, 53, 60, 62, 103, 127
rituals ix, 1, 107

S

self xi, xii, xiii, 2, 6, 9, 10, 11, 12, 17, 18, 19, 22, 26, 27, 37, 43, 44, 45, 47, 55, 59, 60, 72, 76, 78, 83, 84, 85, 97, 102, 103, 104, 111, 112, 118
self-realization 17, 97, 111
spiritualist 5
spiritual liberation xii, 19, 21, 38, 46
stress x, 72
substance xv, 14, 19, 55, 66, 76, 89, 90, 97, 98

T

thinker xiv
third eye 63, 68, 111
Thought xii, xiii, xiv, xv, 3, 5, 6, 7, 8, 11, 13, 14, 18, 26, 27, 28, 29, 30, 31, 32, 34, 36, 37, 38, 40, 41, 42, 43, 45, 46, 47, 48, 50, 51, 52, 54, 55, 58, 59, 60, 61, 63, 75, 76, 77, 83, 84, 85, 86, 90, 91, 96, 98, 99, 101, 102, 103, 104, 113, 114, 115, 123, 130

trance 17, 31
transcendent 13, 89, 111, 114, 115
Truth xii, xiii, 1, 2, 4, 5, 6, 7, 9, 12, 13, 19, 22, 24, 30, 31, 33, 38, 43, 44, 45, 46, 53, 54, 76, 77, 81, 84, 85, 90, 91, 95, 97, 98, 101, 102, 103, 104, 114, 120

U

Ultimate Source of Energy 1, 2, 10, 52
Universal Law xi, xiv, 14, 30, 32, 43, 46, 48, 52, 59, 76, 83, 98, 99, 103, 104
unpretentiously xii

V

vibration xv, 6, 19, 27, 28, 34, 35, 37, 43, 48, 69, 70, 72, 109, 112, 119

W

Word vii, xiv, xv, 1, 2, 3, 14, 20, 29, 31, 33, 34, 36, 37, 42, 43, 47, 54, 55, 59, 60, 62, 64, 70, 75, 76, 90, 95, 96, 97, 99, 113, 114, 119

www.ingramcontent.com/pod-product-compliance
Lightning Source LLC
LaVergne TN
LVHW091530070526
838199LV00001B/6